Dick Pronto

*f*P

THE
CLICKABLE
CORPORATION

*Successful Strategies for
Capturing the Internet Advantage*

JONATHAN ROSENOER
DOUGLAS ARMSTRONG
J. RUSSELL GATES

THE FREE PRESS

THE FREE PRESS
A Division of Simon & Schuster Inc.
1230 Avenue of the Americas
New York, NY 10020

Designed by Carla Bolte

Manufactured in the United States of America

10   9   8   7   6   5   4   3   2   1

Library of Congress Cataloging-in-Publication Data

Rosenoer, Jonathan.
    The clickable corporation : successful strategies for capturing
the internet advantage / by Jonathan Rosenoer, Douglas Armstrong, and
J. Russell Gates.
        p.   cm.
    Includes index.
    1. Business enterprises—Computer networks.   2. Internet (Computer
network)   I. Armstrong, Douglas.   II. Gates, J. Russell   III. Title.
HD30.37.R674   1999
658'.054678—dc21   99-17594
                                                                CIP

ISBN 0–684–85553–4

To Shery, Michal, Nicholas, and Sophie,
from one guy sitting on the beach
who loves you dearly.
—Jonathan Rosenoer

To Betsy, who I know will be a wonderful author,
and to my parents, who gave me every opportunity to succeed.
—Douglas Armstrong

To Pam, Geoffrey, and Megan
for their understanding and support.
—Russ Gates

Contents

Foreword

The financial markets are sending us a message: the process whereby organizations create wealth has changed. As this book makes eminently clear, the Internet is an essential element of that change.

It used to be so simple. You measured your company's worth by the value of its assets, which was largely reflected in its book value. As recently as two decades ago, the ratio of market value to book value was 1. Today, it is more than 4. What happened? Why has the market value of a Microsoft or an Amazon.com soared, while traditional companies have languished? Because Wall Street has recognized that a company's worth today is driven not simply by traditional financial and physical assets but also by the assets of the Information Age.

In the Agrarian Age, those who owned land reaped the benefit. In the Industrial Age, it was those who controlled the means of production and distribution. The engine of wealth creation in the Information Age is assets that are generally not included in book value—we call it the gap in GAAP (generally accepted accounting principles). Customers, alliances, people, and organizational knowledge are the assets that account for the revolution in market value.

The ability to leverage information, to acquire the knowledge necessary to create and distribute new goods and services, is built upon a new form of connectivity. It's called the Internet. It is ubiquitous. It is cost effective. And both of these characteristics will grow with the continued deregulation in telecommunications and the development of global standards. The search for relevant content is accelerating, as are the opportunities for new forms of service. Witness the meteoric rise of companies like Yahoo, organizations dedicated to the new connectivity and leveraging their information assets.

The powerful role played by ".com" in wealth creation today has spurred many companies to consider the impact the Internet will have on their current business models. Barnes & Noble recognized the threat posed by Amazon.com and joined its competitor online. Will supermarkets like Safeway follow suit? Will Yahoo look-alikes come to control the main portals to products, services and business intelligence?

In this book you will find an early scan of the Net's impact on businesses in a wide variety of industries. The examples range from the simple adaptation of Web sites to boost sales to the evolution of whole new business models. All of them grow out of the ubiquitous and increasingly affordable connectivity that is the gift of the Net.

The Clickable Corporation contains ideas and insights that will point readers toward their own Internet-based opportunities for new wealth creation. At the very least, it is sure to make them aware of the potential of the Net as a business tool.

The urgent reality of the Internet is a strategic challenge none of us can afford to ignore. The competitive landscape of the future will inevitably be shaped not so much by the struggles of individual products for market share, but by the battle of business models to serve the same market.

Thomas B. Kelly

Visit our Web site at http://www.arthurandersen.com/clickable

Tom Kelly, the former Managing Partner of Arthur Andersen's Knowledge Enterprises, is Chairman and CEO of Sedona Institute, a newly formed organization dedicated to executive development programs.

Acknowledgments

A number of people and companies provided substantial assistance and support to the content and form of this book. Acknowledgments need to begin with the Arthur Andersen organization, Thomas B. Kelly, and Steve M. Samek. We owe them a great deal of thanks for their support and encouragement.

A debt of gratitude is also owed to specific people at Arthur Andersen whose contributions are of great value to us. Harry Wallace and David Shevenaugh worked with us from the beginning. We received invaluable suggestions from Robert Hiebeler, Brad Carrier, Ray Cheung, and David Sockol. Thanks to all the people at the companies that we interviewed, particularly for their patience with us.

We also received notable assistance from Magdalena Yesil, Shanda Bahles, Geoff Workman, David Jevans, and Pam Stewart, who helped us move from draft to manuscript. Donna Carpenter and the staff at Wordworks, Inc., including Christina Braun, Maurice Coyle, Fred Dillon, Erik Hansen, Susan Higgins, Susannah Ketchum, Martha Lawler, Susanna Margolis, Edward R. McPherson, Jr., Barbara E. Nelson, Toni Porcelli, Cindy Sammons, John Sammons, Juanita Sammons, Jill Sortet, Saul Wisnia, and G. Patton Wright, were instrumental in bringing this book to life. Finally, thanks to our publisher, Paula Duffy, and editor, Bob Wallace, whose direction and guidance was invaluable.

1

The Future Is Only a Click Away

Now that most of us do business on the Internet,
none of us can do business without it.

R emember great travel agents? They were the godsends who saved
us from squandering our time punching telephone buttons. Like
brilliant sleuths, they penetrated mazes of travel gobbledygook, getting
straight answers to the simple question of how we could get from A to Z
and back again.

And then, alas, they began disappearing, victims of turmoil in the
travel industry. But, wonder of wonders, we may have gained something
better. Thanks to the Internet—the world's most useful do-it-yourself
tool—the best travel agent may, in fact, be sitting right in your chair.

The Internet has changed everything. Today, anyone can be his or her
own travel agent, easily locating the best fares, flights, hotels, or car rentals
in a few minutes of tapping away at the keyboard of a personal computer.

Because millions—and more millions each day—routinely access vast banks of travel data at 56K modem speed, customers need not cede control to someone else, as in the past. In a notable shift in power, travelers are increasingly taking charge of the travel business.

So who besides travelers are profiting from this phenomenon? Easy: tens of thousands of Web-savvy businesses, whose customers are the millions of mouse-clicking computer users across the planet. They are clickable corporations—and the topic of this book.

Clickable corporations are dramatically closing the old gap between themselves and their customers. On the Internet, buyers and sellers can achieve nearly instant rapport. Mutual satisfaction is only a few clicks away.

MSN Expedia (www.expedia.com), the online travel service from Microsoft Corporation, offers a compelling example.

Microsoft originally planned a CD-ROM of travel information culled from some twenty printed guides and travel magazines. The company simply wanted a piece of the $200 *million* travel-guide industry, which seemed ripe for a user-friendly alternative to print media.

But Richard Barton, the manager at Microsoft in charge of the project, spotted a bigger opportunity. His idea: Sell not just travel information, but actual travel services online. As he noted, "That's a $200 *billion* industry."

Microsoft's co-founder, chairman, and chief executive officer, William H. Gates III, approved, and Barton established Expedia's Web site. Launched in 1996, it was an instant hit. Within a year, it boasted 150,000 visitors a month; within two years, that figure had risen twenty-fold. Today, net monthly revenues top $12 million.

Just what services MSN Expedia performs for its obviously pleased customers—and just where its burgeoning revenues come from—are detailed in Chapter 2. But Expedia is hardly a special case.

This book argues that the Internet is the business opportunity of the century, an electronic Klondike, a new gold rush for all sorts of companies, provided they can solve the puzzle of how to turn trillions of mouse clicks into solid sales.

In the pages that follow, we profile twenty-five companies that seem to have, in fact, solved the puzzle and opened opportunities for themselves.

But this book is addressed to other companies: the hesitaters. They are the businesses—thousands of them across the globe—that remain dubious, confused, or simply uninformed about the Web's ability to sell their products and services.

If your business is among them, you may have good reason for your reluctance. Maybe you tried the Internet and had a difficult experience. Or maybe you just don't want to fool with something you don't know enough about. Or you hesitate to send your credit card number into the ether.

All are valid reasons—assuming the Web won't be a competitive factor in your industry anytime soon. If that is your assumption, we suggest it is time to think again. In our view, all the evidence confirms that Internet usage will soon—in five years at most—dominate every industry in every corner of the world.

The Web is already a planetary infrastructure, like highways and electricity. Now that many of us do business on it, we argue here that none of us will be able to do business without it.

How long can you afford to hold out? That's really for you to analyze—and carefully. We simply think the time for hesitation was yesterday.

Our own assumption is that most holdouts are either swayed by misconceptions about the Internet or not yet sufficiently briefed about its extraordinary advantages. Let's examine the misconceptions first.

❑ *Nobody makes money on the Web.*

The media's frequent stories about the Internet's profitless companies typically overlook the fact that many currently spend more than they earn, because they are building infrastructures from scratch. Wall Street understands: Many Internet startups boast stock-market valuations in significant multiples of their revenues, giving them easy access to the capital they need to grow.

❑ *It doesn't hurt to wait and see.*

Many companies prefer to let others in their industry break the trail and cope with the headaches that Internet leaders sometimes encounter. That strategy didn't benefit Barnes & Noble, Inc. It simply watched an Internet-only bookseller, Amazon.com, Inc., seize a strong first-mover advantage (and a market capitalization that tops Borders Group, Inc., and Barnes & Noble combined). Now Barnes & Noble is catching up, but not without paying a price.

❑ *Doing business on the Web costs too much.*

It certainly isn't cheap, but many companies say the benefits far outweigh the costs. Autobytel.com, Inc., the leading Internet car-buying site, has seen demand for its services grow from 361,000 purchase orders handled, for all of 1996, to more than 970,000 handled, by the end of the second quarter of 1998. Autobytel.com assures us that its Internet investment has paid for itself many times over. Cisco Systems, Inc., which attributes $500 million savings in annual operating expenses to its networked business model, reports that online sales have resulted in about a 15% increase in account executive and sales engineer productivity. The benefits for Cisco have even spread to the recruiting process, where receiving resumes via the Internet has led to an $8 million recruiting cost reduction.

❏ *Internet customers are vulnerable to theft.*

Some holdouts fear losing customers, who worry that Internet intruders will steal their credit card data. If this were an uncontrollable problem—which it isn't—scores of the nation's biggest companies would not be conducting millions of credit card transactions, safely and smoothly, round the clock, every day of the week.

❏ *Web sites are vulnerable to competitors.*

The perceived fear here is that your site may be picked clean by competitors poaching proprietary information about your customers, products, or services. This isn't the case.

Actually, some Internet companies rather hope their competitors *do* snoop around their Web sites. Autobytel.com and Coldwell Banker Real Estate Corporation, for example, believe that it makes good business sense to let competitors see what you have for sale.

❏ *The Internet isn't big enough.*

More than 100 million people are already online. At the current growth rate, that number will reach one billion within five years—an order of acceleration and connectivity never seen before. And even in five years, the vast majority of the world's people won't yet have owned computers, much less have gone online, ensuring future Internet growth for years to come. If that isn't a mass market, what is?

So these misconceptions have been dismissed—or at least addressed. What, then, are the Internet's advantages?

The twenty-five businesses we profile in the book show us that the Internet offers eight distinct advantages—most of which may seem, at first glance, to be variations on the ways you have dealt with customers for years. But these ways are not the same. The difference is in the details. A Web transaction doesn't necessarily start with or involve salespeople, direct mail, or catalogs, much less a store. Even customer behavior is different.

Internet customers expect to deal with a fast, reliable, easy-to-use interface. They expect flawless products and services. They can easily compare yours to others by clicking on your competitors' Web sites. Dealing with them profitably requires new strategies and tactics, all detailed in the pages ahead.

Here are the eight Internet advantages we have drawn from the hard-won experience of our twenty-five companies.

❏ *Information*

The Internet enables you to provide information about your products or services in whatever detail at whatever time your customers desire it. Instead of waiting in line to talk to a salesperson, or hunting through a catalog, a customer can immediately learn all he or she wants to know about specifications, costs, terms of service, and compatibility with other products.

For its part, a Web-savvy business can provide the pearls to satisfy even its most demanding customers. It can also offer different routes by which customers can access information—according to manufacturer, style, and color, for example—and allow users to download and print that information. In Chapter 2, Autobytel.com, Bloomberg L.P., and MSN Expedia all demonstrate the advantage information provides.

❏ *Choice*

Web customers aren't only particular. They also can easily click to your competitor's site. It is, after all, a lot simpler than driving to another store, or even walking across the mall. To counter this problem, you must offer greater variety and choice. The Internet makes it possible, because Web sites have none of the space and inventory limits of traditional retail businesses.

On the other hand, you have to organize your site in a way that doesn't overwhelm customers with too many choices. They need an efficient search engine—and clear categories—to narrow their options. In Chapter 3, we look at three companies that have done this well: Barnes & Noble, Coldwell Banker, and Marshall Industries, Inc.

❏ *Convenience*

The Internet is the ultimate convenience store. It is always on open, not only for taking orders but also for tracking deliveries, receiving shipments, even enabling customers to communicate in their native tongues. For Peapod, Inc., the online grocer, convenience takes the form of a site that allows customers to match home deliveries to their work schedules. In Chapter 4, Peapod, Federal Express Corporation, Pitney Bowes, Inc., and 1-800-Flowers, Inc., all demonstrate the value of Web convenience.

❏ *Customization*

The Internet gives businesses a unique capacity to tailor products or services to fit the needs of customers. On many sites, customers are encouraged to design their own products and services—and shown a graphic image of the results.

Dell Computer Corporation not only offers guidelines for possible configurations, but also helps customers order directly from the supplier that makes, say, Dell's computer monitors. In Chapter 5, we look at how both Dell and Cisco Systems, Inc., have made customization a high priority on their Web sites.

❏ Savings

You will never have less labor-intensive sales than those you clinch on the Internet. But your cost savings go beyond the absence of sales representatives. You can use the Web to streamline processes, eliminate organizational barriers, and more efficiently manage your supply chain. The results: higher revenues, lower production and distribution costs, a chance to pass savings along to customers and increase market share, and, in Cisco's case, increase customer satisfaction. In Chapter 6, Northwest Airlines Company, and BMG Direct, Inc., illustrate the value of passing along savings to customers.

❏ Community

In times past, community was a function of geography, centered in the churches, schools, and living rooms of your hometown. The automobile and telephone changed that, and now the Internet is transforming it as well. Suddenly, people from all over the world with a common interest in estate planning, women's rights, or nursing homes are meeting and creating new communities online.

Alert companies are providing these new communities with resources, such as guest speakers and chat rooms and otherwise attracting them as another online business opportunity. In Chapter 7, we profile some of the Internet's best community creators, including GeoCities, Inc., Purple Moon, Inc., SeniorNet, Inc., and Women.com Networks.

❏ *Entertainment*

Whether you're selling jets or geraniums, the Web offers all sorts of ways to attract customers by entertaining them. Some companies provide interactive access to games, music, and sports on their Web sites, and on the customers' own terms. On the Internet site of the International Business Machines Corporation, for example, viewers were able to choose their preferred camera angles for the Wimbledon tennis championships. Chapter 8 shows how Brøderbund Software, Inc., Berkeley Systems, Inc., CBS, Inc., and IBM are all using entertainment to promote their products and services.

❏ *Trust*

When the only handshake available is between modems, how much trust can be found in an online relationship? Web-wise companies emphasize secure technology—encryption, for example—to make sure that the information exchanged is kept private. They also bend over backwards to make sure their Internet pages are available, welcoming, easy to use, and fast.

By nurturing customer confidence in sensitive transactions, these companies add essential value to their products and services, and that translates into increased revenues. This is definitely true for Metropolitan Life Insurance Company, Wells Fargo & Company, and Charles Schwab & Company, which are the companies profiled in Chapter 9.

The twenty-five organizations we examine in this book were chosen for a variety of reasons. Some were leaders, some were followers. Some were proactive, others were forced to react. Some are well known, others are emerging or are in relatively niche markets. The common factor is that they all exemplify one or more of the eight essential benefits that companies seeking to leverage the Internet deliver to their customers. Indeed, some may deliver all eight. Does this mean they all will be successful in the long term or that they are, or will be, better than their competitors? In some cases, perhaps, but it takes a lot more than just a successful Internet strategy to be successful, and we'll leave this determination to the best judge—the customer.

The case histories can help guide you toward building a successful Web strategy that will increase your return to your customers, shareholders, and business partners. But the case histories will only provide ideas. You will need to invest a considerable amount of time and energy to turn your ideas into successful and sustainable solutions. You'll need to involve many parts of your organization in this process if you want your solution to be truly integrated into your business and business strategies, so don't even think of throwing it over the transom to be completed by your information technology team. Yes, you will need to make a host of technology decisions, but your decisions will need to be broader in scope than Web servers, HTML, and protocols. You have to determine your company's core business objectives, with an eye to what your competitors are doing and where your market is headed. What products or services do you want to sell? Which of your processes can be improved by conducting them on the Internet? What customers do you hope to attract and serve? What do your customers and business partners want, expect, or even demand in terms of customer care and customer service? What level of financial and personnel support can you commit? What level of online sophistication do you wish to incorporate into your site? What level of leadership will be required to move the project to a successful conclusion? What costs can we remove from the channel?

Once you have decided to pursue business on the Internet, you will face additional concerns, such as figuring out site-building logistics and integrating new technology with your existing technologies and business processes. You may also need to consider some new business risks that you may not have considered before—privacy, security, performance, and scalability among the most prevalent. Depending on your business, you may face new and unforeseen regulatory or tax issues. And once your solution is up and running, you will have to make sure it gets the continued marketing support it will need.

"A lot of companies think it's a technical problem. You know, if we put up our entry on the Web, we'll get the business," Peter Solvik, chief information officer for Cisco Systems, told us. "But if you don't promote and support and market your site, people aren't going to use it."

You will find down-to-earth, practical insights on these and other issues in the next eight chapters. No matter what business you are in or where your company is on the Internet adoption curve (see graph on page 24), issues of designing, building, and improving an Internet presence are sure to be faced by your company. We suggest that sooner is better.

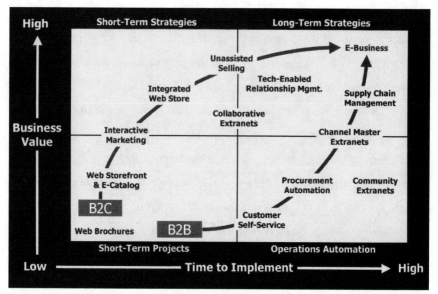

Internet Adoption Curve

Source: GartnerGroup, *B2B vs. B2C Paths to E-commerce Success,* October 1998.

2

Click with Information

Share your knowledge.
Reap the benefits.

———————————

What is the information advantage?

Your parents thought it belonged to the Sears, Roebuck & Company catalog, a lap-bruising monster crammed with mail-order goodies that Americans perused all year long until the next issue arrived. Though it probably outweighed some of its readers, the Sears catalog was a brilliant marketing tool. It told consumers precisely what they needed to know in an era when the nearest department stores might be miles or even counties away.

To this day, the Sears information advantage still inspires direct merchants as diverse as Lillian Vernon Corporation and L. L. Bean, Inc., who have built their businesses on print catalogs. But the paper medium, we suggest, is the wave of the past. To more and more Internet users, print catalogs are fodder for the nearest recycling bin.

Today's consumers have grown accustomed to instant responses from all kinds of computerized devices, ranging from automated teller machines to microwave ovens. The Web conditions people to expect the same from virtually all businesses. The key to their expectations is how fast and how well any company satisfies their hunger for reliable, usable information.

The climate could not be better for clickable corporations. Consider this: If shoppers want to know everything imaginable about your better mousetrap, you can assume they are comparing it to other mousetraps, and you then have a way to outsell your competitors—outdo them in answering your customers' questions.

Just pile on the facts, please—full disclosure on price, quality, reliability. And we do mean everything. The more you tell, the more you create an information advantage that results in sales. And the more you tell about your products or services on your Internet site, the more your information advantage becomes unbeatable.

The Web is the perhaps best way to provide fast answers using information that is inclusive, organized, customized, and constantly updated. One caveat, though: Badly organized information, to say nothing of just bad information, can alienate customers and destroy your advantage.

The trick is to send rifle-shot responses to customers' specific needs. Whether those customers need data about components, costs, deliveries, or warranties, the Web-wise business sifts through seas of information for the pearl that will satisfy its most demanding buyer.

The companies we examine in this chapter have all found ways to capture the information advantage. Car buyers can click on Autobytel.com,

Inc.'s site and rapidly locate the deal that best suits them. Visitors to the Bloomberg L.P. site get up-to-the-minute news on stocks and bonds as well as economic analyses and informative reports. Business travelers or vacationers can plan their next trip by clicking on Microsoft Corporation's MSN Expedia, which seems to know so much about travel that it probably could have whipped off Marco Polo's itinerary faster than it takes most people to spell Xanadu.

Autobytel.com Clicks with Information

Think of Autobytel.com (www.autobytel.com) as a matchmaking service for people and cars. Based in Irvine, California, the company was founded in 1995 by a former car dealer, Peter Ellis. Its mission: give prospective car buyers access to the data they need to choose the automobile that is right for them. Then connect these people to car dealers, who offer no-haggle, competitive prices and convenient—often one-hour or less—delivery of vehicles.

Autobytel.com has fulfilled its mission by making the most of information. The company estimates that 20 to 30 percent of its referrals to car dealers actually result in sales. That success rate has prompted more than 2,700 auto retailers in North America alone to pay monthly fees to be part of Autobytel.com's network.

In its early stages, Autobytel.com used focus groups to determine what people wanted when it came to buying a car. These groups included many women, who, Ellis suspected, disliked the traditional hard sell and haggling. Their responses revealed that buyers wanted accurate information—delivered in a nonconfrontational environment. The Web is that environment.

"In the three-plus years the site has been up," says Mark Lorimer, president and chief executive officer of Autobytel.com, Inc., "our value proposition has basically stayed the same—it has not and will not change."

When prospective car buyers log on to www.autobytel.com, they can review a wealth of auto-related information. For instance, customers might use the online research library to study data supplied by car manufacturers, as well as articles and studies that may be critical of specific models, such as those published in *Consumer Reports* or *Esquire*. They can browse through hundreds of photos of every make and model. They can check out prices in the *Kelly Blue Book, Edmund's Car Buying Guide, Intellichoice,* and other reference guides. They can research the latest incentives and rebates through Autobytel.com's *Weekly AutoMarket Report*. They can even request online insurance quotes; apply for state-specific warranty coverage, or mechanical breakdown insurance; and even finance the car of their choice. Autobytel.com also offers the Mobalist Rewards Program, which allows car buyers to earn unlimited rewards towards the purchase of their next car through a network of participating Web retailers.

For those who want the process to be fast and easy, Autobytel.com's site offers a simple search—called Car Selector—that asks customers their price range and what features are important to them. It then quickly calls up vehicles that meet their needs. It cuts through information overload and saves all those hours spent cruising showrooms.

Customers who know what vehicle they want can simply enter the FasTrak portion of the site, click on their choice, and indicate when they wish to purchase it. An image of the model appears on screen with a checklist of options, including interior and exterior colors, power windows, cruise control, and sound systems. As customers select different options, the dealer invoice and manufacturer's suggested retail price for the vehicles change. What is created in the end is a customized purchase request, an "online window sticker" that is ready for direct routing to an Autobytel.com-trained manager at an Autobytel.com Accredited Dealership.

Customers type in their zip code and send the purchase request and an optional finance or lease application. The purchase request is then sent to their local Autobytel.com dealer, who calls within twenty-four hours to set up delivery time. According to Autobytel.com guidelines the dealer is required to contact the customer within that twenty-four-hour window and offer the lowest price at which that dealer is willing to sell the car.

Through its financial-services subsidiary, Autobytel.com Acceptance Corporation (ABTAC), the company offers competitive finance rates and a quick, painless online application and approval. Finance and lease applications are forwarded to participating lending institutions for same-day processing. Once approved, the financing agreement is sent to the Accredited Dealer, who explains terms to the customer. All of the details about financing can be taken care of before the customer takes delivery of the car.

Autobytel.com's network of over 2,700 Accredited Dealerships is further testament to the company's smart use of information. The company has developed Web technology, called Dealer Real Time, that smoothly integrates its own business processes with those of its affiliated dealerships. This system works so well that customers sometimes receive calls from dealers before they have logged off the site.

To keep this system running efficiently, Autobytel requires dealers to meet rigorous accreditation standards that include a history of outstanding customer service, no-haggle fair-price policies, and a substantial inventory of vehicles.

Because Autobytel.com sends ready-to-buy customers to its dealers, the company needs assurance that vehicles will be available when customers want them. Failure to comply with Autobytel.com's policy of contacting customers within twenty-four hours of an inquiry may result in the loss of accreditation.

Once it admits a new Accredited Dealer to its network, Autobytel.com provides free training for Autobytel.com's managers, including an introduction to the Internet. After all, dealers have to be as Web-wise as the customers they serve.

Conducting regional training sessions each month throughout the United States, Autobytel.com makes sure that even those trainees without much computer experience can learn to work comfortably with its customers. The company also provides regular refresher courses to keep its dealers up to date with the latest Internet developments.

Autobytel.com hopes to have as many as 3,500 dealerships in their North American network. "We'll grow as fast as we can find dealers who have bought into the process and are ready to deliver to our customers the service they want," Lorimer explains. "That's what we're ultimately here for—to provide our customers with the information they need to easily complete the buying process."

During 1995, Autobytel.com's network of Accredited Dealers received more than 50,000 purchase inquiries. The following year that number increased to 361,000, and by the third quarter of 1997 it had recorded over one million customers. By the end of the second quarter of 1998, Autobytel.com had clocked 971,681 purchase requests for that year alone, 25 percent of which were estimated to translate into actual sales. That added up to $1.5 billion in Web commerce during the second quarter of 1998 alone.

❑ *How Autobytel.com clicks with information:*

1. By providing a trusting, secure environment in which customers can gather and evaluate information.
2. By giving customers a number of ways—key-word search, browsing by subject, hot links to other sources of data—to gather and focus the information they want.
3. By connecting customers to dealers, who are informed of customers' needs and then sustain the trusting, secure environment once the transaction goes offline.

Bloomberg Clicks with Information

As a trading partner at Salomon Brothers Investing, Michael R. Bloomberg knew the advantage of *receiving* the right information at the right time. As founder, president, and chief executive officer of Bloomberg L.P. (www.bloomberg.com), he knows the advantage of *delivering* the right information at the right time.

Bloomberg was the head of equity trading at Salomon Brothers, a position that gave him special insights into the information needs of traders. The 1981 merger between Salomon and Phibro Corporation prompted his departure. The thirty-nine-year-old Bloomberg pocketed $10 million as part of his severance package. Then the fiery Wall Street maverick decided to start his own company.

He founded New York-based Innovative Marketing Systems, investing $4 million to design a computer-based system that could gather, analyze, and disseminate market information in a format easily accessible by traders. The result was a prototype of the Bloomberg terminal, a device that offered users the ability to access proprietary market data whenever they needed it.

When he demonstrated his system to senior managers at investment giant Merrill Lynch and Company, Inc., they were impressed enough to offer him a deal: Install twenty terminals at Merrill Lynch headquarters in New York and receive $30 million in exchange for 30 percent of the infant company.

Over the next several years, Bloomberg developed ways to offer his customers increasing amounts of information on their dedicated terminals. The earliest machines gave users the ability to readily compare securities, but, to distinguish itself from competitors, the company began offering new analytical tools, which Bloomberg himself designed.

The company's mainstay has long been the so-called Bloomberg box, a stand-alone computer terminal that delivers stock quotations, analyses, and other financial news. Bloomberg customers pay up to $1,200 a month for its services. The company leased its first box in 1982—in 1998, more than 140,000 people in ninety-one countries were using Bloomberg terminals.

Today, though, the company is better known for the information it provides than for the hardware clients use to access it. The public's embrace of the Internet, however, has given "civilian" computer users the opportunity to access financial information on their own. Some skeptics predicted dire consequence for Bloomberg, but, rather than fizzling out, the company has diversified and prospered.

The Internet seems ideal for fulfilling Bloomberg's goal of delivering information the moment it becomes available. Its Web site differentiates it from its competitors by interpreting this information with astonishing savvy and the wisdom born of twenty years of experience. Launched in December 1995, Bloomberg Online is a compilation of news and analyses based on the company's unmatched information-gathering prowess—all wrapped into a sensible, user-friendly format.

"There's a lot of data out there on the Internet, obviously more than any single person can read," says Jon Fram, general manager of new media. "Bloomberg's challenges are to help customers find content over clutter, to present data in a comprehensive manner. We started Bloomberg Online when the concept wasn't understood or even in consumers' line of vision. What was our niche yesterday, however, is in the mainstream today."

In addition to advertisements on its Web site, Bloomberg derives its main Internet income from users who choose to subscribe to additional proprietary services online. Sophisticated and detailed online analysis has kept subscriptions to the Bloomberg box and the company's other services steady. Thanks in large part to its Web presence—and an ever-expanding number of multimedia offerings—the company's annual revenue topped $1 billion in 1997.

"What the Internet does is give us access to a broad consumer market that previously was just not available," explains Fram. "The average consumer in the United States has more invested in stocks than in home equity, so an interest in financial assets is the highest of all money needs. Information is the unit that determines the value and power of those assets. And the power Bloomberg offers customers is information, which in turn powers us to be profitable."

Casual visitors to the Bloomberg Web site can access first-level information and services for free: up-to-the-minute market news, stock quotes, tax forms, and charts to help calculate and better understand mortgages, education payments, and 401(K)s. Full subscribers get detailed analyses of stocks and other securities, as well as portions of *Bloomberg Personal,* a monthly personal-finance magazine. The site, in short, serves as a major resource for capturing and using financial knowledge and know-how.

To enhance Bloomberg's services and brand, the company complements its Web site by disseminating news and data through more traditional channels. Launched in 1990, Bloomberg News employs nine hundred reporters and offers syndicated coverage of business, politics, sports, and entertainment to more than 850 newspapers worldwide. Its twenty-four-hour-a-day television network broadcasts major news stories (with a business concentration) in seven languages, and its radio network includes one hundred worldwide affiliates. Holdings also include *Bloomberg Personal* and a publishing affiliate that produces both personal and professional books.

❏ *How Bloomberg clicks with information:*

1. By developing a format that makes information accessible—and relevant—to users.
2. By offering customers unique and sophisticated analyses of information.
3. By delivering information the instant it becomes available.
4. By developing an extensive information-gathering network that allows it to offer information no one else has.
5. By developing different channels for disseminating information to different audiences.

Expedia Clicks with Information

Yearning to watch the sunset off the coast of Antarctica? Dream of traveling the ancient Silk Road through Asia? Or do you just want to find a reasonably priced hotel within walking distance of Picadilly Circus? MSN Expedia (www.expedia.com), Microsoft's Web site devoted to travel, might well be your first destination. Equal parts travel agent and guidebook, this is a site that truly lives up to the Internet promise of putting the customer in charge.

"We're aiming our product at the person who wants to take control," says Richard Barton, manager of Microsoft's travel business unit and the man behind the Web site. "The people who want to delegate decision making to someone else are not our core customers."

During the early 1990s, Microsoft planned to enter the travel business by taking the CD-ROM route. It was looking for a piece of the $200 million guidebook industry. "It was going to run into the millions of dollars to produce the thing. So instead of trying to get a piece of the $200 million travel guide business, I thought, why not try and go online and sell travel? That's a $200 billion business."

Barton shared his idea with Microsoft's CEO Bill Gates at a strategy session in late 1994, and Gates agreed. Work began immediately on a travel site that would be part of the Microsoft Network (MSN), the Internet service provider the company was developing for release in 1995. It was soon decided, however, that the site should be autonomous and free to users.

A unit of Microsoft's Interactive Media Group, MSN Expedia was launched in October 1996. It was an immediate success, with travelers finding it a welcome alternative to relying on friends, agents, and guidebooks that are often outdated by the time they go to press. Recognized by Media Metrix as 1997's fastest-growing travel site, MSN Expedia had sales of $12 million in January of 1998 alone. In 1997 *Internet Life* called it the "Coolest Site of the Year," and *PC Week* crowned it as the best site on the Internet.

The success of the site was hardly accidental. Using focus groups, Microsoft designers determined that an effective and speedy site was far more important than an attractive one. They also ran labs where volunteers used a prototype MSN Expedia site to purchase tickets. Barton's team watched through one-way mirrors and quickly realized the importance of guiding users through the process. They intentionally silenced the bells and whistles in favor of delivering information quickly and clearly.

But where would that information come from? The big-time players in the travel industry—airline companies, hotel chains, car rental agencies—had huge quantities of data stored in proprietary mainframes. Microsoft began forming alliances with companies such as Northwest, Continental, and KLM. It knew it would need strategic partnerships if it was going to offer consumers real control of designing and implementing their travel plans.

Barton was amazed at how quickly the site caught on with the public. In its first month MSN Expedia had 150,000 visitors and sales of $2 million. The company quickly realized that it was crucial to have a team of backup phone representatives. Users liked having the information they needed to find the best deals and create their own adventures, but they still wanted someone to confirm a reservation, issue a ticket, or verify a connection.

"We didn't anticipate how important phone reps were going to be to the whole sales process," says Barton. "Getting people to push the 'buy' button to book a trip or purchase a service is very difficult. Sometimes a little help from a rep goes a long way."

The company has continually refined the software to help it define its customers—one at a time. "We built software capable of growing smarter about the individual customer, not the average customer," explains Barton. "With our Faretracker service we ask each customer to name three cities he or she would travel to on a moment's notice if the price was right. Then we can e-mail that customer fare information on those cities once a week— and if a special deal opens up, we e-mail immediately."

MSN Expedia markets itself as a "one-stop service shop," a claim supported by its range of services, which enable customers to:

1. Access the lowest airline fares, both at the site and by e-mail.
2. See if seats are available on a specific flight.
3. Determine the availability of and then reserve rental cars at any airport in the world.
4. Use a directory of more than 38,000 hotels worldwide to confirm room availability, prices, and pertinent information. Some rooms can even be viewed digitally.
5. Confirm the arrival time and gate of flights.
6. Request a window seat, order a special in-flight meal, get frequent flyer miles, and generally fine tune every aspect of their travel plans.
7. Use specialized tools such as the Flight Wizard, Car Wizard, or Hotel Wizard to plan trips and automatically qualify for special promotions.

MSN Expedia, in short, empowers members to be their own travel agents. If Jane Jones wants to find the cheapest flight from Boston to Los Angeles next Tuesday, she simply tells Flight Wizard. Within minutes, MSN Expedia informs her of the lowest fare—along with aircraft model, ticket restrictions, meal information, and total price with taxes. After choosing her flight, Jane simply clicks and the ticket is booked.

Once the flight information is saved to Jane's personal itinerary, it's on to the Hotel Wizard. Does she want to stay out near the airport, or closer to the Getty, where she has a reservation for Wednesday morning? Splurge on the room or save a little money so she can shop Montana Avenue? An indoor pool is a must to swim off the jet lag. The Hotel Wizard quickly gives her the information she needs to make her decision. Turns out the Beverly Hills Hotel is having a last-minute sale—she can get a suite for the price of a room *and* do Montana Avenue. Another click and the room is booked. Jane only has one question left: How did anyone live before MSN Expedia?

But airlines and hotels are only the beginning of what MSN Expedia offers. Its Travel Network helps members search for cruises; special interest trips for golfers, chocolate lovers, or Anglophiles; resorts that cater to honeymooners or seniors; spas that specialize in post-facelift recuperation; and even for unglamorous but often critical bus schedules. Users can even do some pre-trip cybershopping at more than thirty different stores that specialize in travel merchandise. Then there's the World Guide, a 14,000-page compendium of up-to-the-minute information on more than three hundred different regions of the world. This unique feature also provides links to maps, photographs, and transportation tips.

Want more? MSN Expedia has compiled over fifteen thousand articles on the world's great cultural attractions; provides links to www.sidewalk.com—a site that lists entertainment events around the globe—and ten thousand other travel-related Web sites; and features 360-degree panoramic photo essays of different locales in *MSN Expedia Magazine.*

MSN Expedia profits from three revenue streams. Acting as a virtual travel agent, it collects commissions from airlines, hotels, car rental companies, and the like—charging less than the typical 8 to 12 percent commission. Travel companies are interested in working with MSN Expedia because of its large and affluent membership, many of whom travel frequently.

A second major revenue stream is advertising. Companies buy banner ads at a cost of approximately $40 CPM (cost per thousand impressions). Since the site gets three million visitors a month, companies are assured of tremendous exposure. Microsoft also charges hotels for an enhanced Hotel Wizard listing that includes a written description, map, and photographs.

The third revenue producer is distribution fees from partner companies that connect to the site. "Someone who is running a cruise site or an adventure travel site or a train travel site will buy a connection to us," explains Barton. "We have a number of such deals, which form the Expedia Travel Network."

From Barton's point of view, MSN Expedia represents a fundamental power shift from provider to customer. "Basically, power has been migrating out towards the customer over the last hundred years," Barton says. "And what's more powerful than having a tool that allows you access to previously unavailable information?"

MSN Expedia is not only letting travelers chart their own paths, it is drawing the map of e-commerce's future.

❏ *How Expedia clicks with information:*

1. By giving consumers access to previously unavailable, or difficult-to-access information.

2. By allowing customers to take control of the travel-planning process.

3. By focusing on delivering information clearly—not with a lot of frills.

How You Can Click with Information

- By narrowing your focus. With so much information out there, no company can be all things to all people. Develop a niche, then offer depth over breadth.

- By distilling information. We're all drowning in data. Save your customers a lot of time and effort by extracting what's really important.

- By showcasing what's important. Let your customers know the benefit of specific information before you present the information itself.

- By testing prototypes. Your target customers can help you identify the kinds and categories of information that are most important to them.

- By giving customers access to information that was heretofore unavailable to them. That way, they can manage their own transactions.

- By valuing accessibility over visual effects. Information-hungry customers prefer uncluttered Web sites to those dominated by graphics. Use focus groups to help you identify distracting clutter and flag design attributes that may drive away customers.

- By supporting your site. Customers need offline advice from you, and it is the wise company that provides it. Set up a toll-free telephone number, and staff it with knowledgeable customer-service representatives, salespeople, and the like.

3

Click with Choice

Help customers make a choice.
Watch them choose you.

Free of all physical limits, with premises that exist only in the customer's imagination, the clickable corporation boosts sales by offering a huge and potentially infinite variety of products and services.

But too much choice may be no choice. Consumers aren't gluttons. Sheer excess confuses and drives them away. They want the right choice, for the right price, right now.

The Web's winners give customers something far more helpful than vast warehouses stuffed with dizzying stacks of unopened cartons. They work hard to help each customer arrive quickly at the best choice, bar none.

Who has the choice advantage?

In this chapter, three companies—Barnes & Noble, Inc., Marshall Industries, Inc., and Coldwell Banker Real Estate Corporation—show

how to use the Internet to handle customer choice persuasively and profitably.

Though Barnes & Noble sells one product—books—it stocks hundreds of thousands of titles, a problem in choice management that the chain's Web site is determined to master.

Electronic parts seller Marshall Industries offers an enormous number of products, as well as services, that make it one of the world's biggest distributors.

The realtors of Coldwell Banker invite online customers to inspect a few houses that precisely meet their specifications. The customers can happily disregard all the thousands of other houses from which Coldwell picked theirs. They need only sit quietly in front of their monitors and ponder.

No more slogging through real estate ads printed in miniscule type. No more endless drives in real estate agents' cars to houses you would not dream of buying. No more confusion. Just click on your next perfect home and go have a celebratory dinner.

Barnes & Noble Clicks with Choice

One of the great challenges for any business is to offer products that match customers' interests and needs. No one knows this better than the people of Barnes & Noble, Inc. (www.barnesandnoble.com). With $3 billion in annual revenues, it is the preeminent brand name in global bookselling. Since March 1997, the company has offered its wares online at barnesandnoble.com. The goal of the site is to match customers with books, and the choice is mind-boggling—more than 2.5 million titles, all at a competitive price.

During the 1990s, Barnes & Noble revolutionized the book business by opening some five hundred superstores, comfy emporiums where customers can browse, chat, lounge, nibble, and, oh yes, buy books. These stores account for more than 80 percent of Barnes & Noble's annual revenues.

But this dynamo is hardly resting on its superstores. While the largest of the stores boasts about 175,000 titles, Barnes & Noble's Web site features ten times that number—more than two million titles—on its (virtual) shelves. And it offers them less expensively, even as it reaches out to customers anywhere in the world twenty-four hours a day.

The Internet transforms Barnes & Noble into a cornucopia of choice that a reader can sample from the comfort of his or her living room. Interested in the history of the fava bean? Obsessed with eighteenth-century Brazilian poetry? Worried about where to put your money? Barnesandnoble.com can lead you to just the right book.

It can also offer reviews of the book, take you onto a Web page or into a chat room devoted solely to your favorite author or interest, make you a member of a virtual book group, and, of course, tell you the price of any given book, then sell it to you. It is no exaggeration to say that barnesandnoble.com has mastered the art of clicking with choice.

How? The Web site begins by dividing its list of titles into categories—everything from astrology to alternative medicine to action-adventure. "Our editorial staff expands the features of those categories," explains David Palmieri, director of new business development at barnesandnoble.com, "so that if the customer is interested in specific subject areas—what we call 'bookshelves' of relevant titles—we can help that customer access the choices he or she wants probably in less than a minute."

Customers can also narrow their choices with the site's search engine. To begin a search, a visitor types in an author's name, the book's title, or general information on the subject. Presto, the site either finds the specific book or offers an array of choices relating to a particular subject. The company maintains a physical inventory of 750,000 titles at its warehouse in New Jersey. These represent 95 to 98 percent of all online purchases. A well-oiled distribution network puts most orders in the mail within 24 hours.

How does Barnes & Noble capture its audience to begin with? An alliance with America Online, Inc. (AOL) is one way. As the exclusive AOL bookseller, barnesandnoble.com is prominently displayed before twelve million AOL members whenever they sign on. This accounts for 30 to 40 percent of Web sales. "As more and more people come online," Palmieri predicts, "they will be looking for brands that they know, and we want to be there when they get there. Our partnership with AOL, therefore, made sense from the start. We're probably the most integrated commerce relationship that AOL has ever had."

Another part of the company's Internet strategy involves affiliating itself with several thousand other complementary sites. The company is the exclusive online bookseller of *The New York Times Book Review*—readers can instantly order a book after reading its review. In addition, the Web site provides content for the online book pages of *USA Today* and Cable News Network (CNN), as well as offering users the opportunity to place an order. In business and finance, barnesandnoble.com is the bookseller for the CBS Marketwatch site. Similar arrangements exist with the online divisions of ESPN, The Walt Disney Company, and the Discovery Channel.

How did Barnes & Noble create this network of affiliates, which allows it to focus on different market segments? After studying its major online competitors, including Amazon.com, the company committed approximately $35 million to create and maintain the Web site. It knew an early infusion of capital was essential. It used its strong brand name to attract its network of affiliates. It also established distribution channels, planned inventory, and built connections to publishers.

For the latter part of 1997, the site reported revenues of $15 million. Support remains strong. Leonard Riggio, Barnes & Noble's founder, chairman, and chief executive officer, has committed $10 million a year for the next four years just to maintain the company's exclusive affiliation with America Online. Palmieri says the company expects such partnerships to produce 25 to 35 percent of all its online revenues. By offering a virtual, virtually unlimited range of choices, barnesandnoble.com is determined to make itself the Web site of choice for readers around the world.

❏ *How Barnes & Noble clicks with choice:*

1. By giving customers new ways to make choices, such as providing book reviews and suggesting titles that fit a profile created by previous purchases.
2. By leveraging a variety of partnership channels to provide potential customers.
3. By pointing readers to choices they didn't even know existed.
4. By connecting readers to each other, thereby exposing them to new authors and interests.

Marshall Industries Clicks with Choice

Few companies have done a better job providing choice than Marshall Industries, Inc. (www.marshall.com), an electronic components distributor based in El Monte, California. In 1994, it became one of the first distributors to go online, making a major financial and manpower commitment to doing business on the Internet. President and chief executive officer Robert Rodin cites the company's Web site as one of the reasons the organization—which posted $1.7 billion in revenue during 1998—has doubled its productivity, tripled its growth, and cut costs substantially.

Visitors to the site can search more than 250,000 products by part number, manufacturer, or product description, and, if they have questions or concerns, they can talk to company technicians in interactive chat sessions. Upon finding what they want, they can order it by credit card or purchase order. And they can track shipments and determine approximate time of arrival.

Founded in 1954, Marshall has become a leader in supplying semiconductors, microprocessors, and circuit boards to high-technology companies around the world. The company also performs valuable services such as component testing and assembly. Rodin joined the company in 1983, quickly rising through the sales and marketing ranks until he was named chief executive in 1992 at the age of thirty-eight.

At that time, Marshall began its initiative to leverage online technology. The company began by supplying laptop computers to all salespeople. If a salesperson couldn't answer a customer's question, he or she queried Marshall's database by modem—and 95 percent of the time came up with an answer on the spot. Marshall's virtual network was effective, but it didn't capture the choice advantage. For that, Marshall needed a Web site.

Www.marshall.com was officially launched in July 1994. Essentially an online catalog without ordering capabilities, the site was popular with engineers, who used it to retrieve information and specifications on products. Later that same year, the company added an order-processing system. And in May 1995, NetSeminars—audio (and sometimes video) lectures by industry leaders—became a regular feature of the site. Customers and suppliers worldwide could interact with the speakers through an online question-and-answer feature. These lectures became so popular that they were spun off onto their own site, one of twenty-six now under the company's umbrella.

What makes Marshall's site really stand out from the many online catalogs is the incredible sophistication of its search engines. An Interactive Selector Guide allows users to type in the exact product parameters (in order of importance) that they are seeking—everything from density and data width to access speed and chip configuration. If a certain parameter isn't necessary, the Selector Guide lets the user know and automatically removes it from the search criteria. If more than one part meets the user's requirements, a complete list of all the possibilities pops up. And, perhaps most impressively, if no part meets the parameters of the search, the selector guide chooses a "best match."

Aware that not all its Internet visitors possess the same degree of technological expertise, Marshall makes it easy. The guide breaks down the various product types available—showing, for instance, that among the semiconductors available are linear, logic, and application-specific devices. When searching by part description, the database finds every part containing the characters inputted. If a user types in "tape reel" and is actually looking for "axial reeling tape," the database will call up the correct product as one possibility. And in those cases when a user still needs help, there is a twenty-four-hour chat room manned by Marshall employees ready to answer all questions.

Skeptics frequently ask Rodin what the return is on his $2-million-a-year Internet investment. His answer reflects the confidence that he has both in the Internet and in the advantage of choice. "I look at the Internet as another marketplace," Rodin says. "If I were to move my business into France tomorrow, I know it would take me some time to establish my identity, my equity, and my company. I would be front-loading with people, advertising, and saying to myself, 'I'm going to be in this marketplace for life, so I have to build my infrastructure, campaign, and presence here.' It's no different with the Internet. When we made these changes to our company, we were doing only a half billion dollars in sales rather than the $1.6 billion we now do. There's no good time to make the move to the Internet, but who can afford to ignore a new marketplace?"

❏ *How Marshall Industries clicks with choice:*

1. By adding intelligence to the choice process.
2. By providing expert advice so customers can make effective choices.
3. By building on a strong brand.
4. By designing incredibly sophisticated and precise search engines.

Coldwell Banker Clicks with Choice

The average homebuyer visits a number of houses before making a decision—a time-consuming, inconvenient, and inefficient process. Talented real estate agents work to understand what buyers want in a house—and then show them only properties that meet those needs. That's the principle behind Parsippany, New Jersey–based real estate franchiser Coldwell Banker's Web site (www.coldwellbanker.com). This savvy interactive tool is designed to determine what buyers want and then show it to them, all from the comfort of their current homes.

Established in San Francisco shortly after the great earthquake in 1906, Coldwell Banker today comprises more than 2,900 independently owned and operated offices throughout the United States, Canada, Puerto Rico, the Caribbean, Bermuda, and Mexico. The work force totals more than 69,000 brokers and sales associates. In 1997, *Franchise Times, Entrepreneur,* and *Success* magazines all voted Coldwell Banker number one in real estate services.

Coldwell Banker launched its original Web site in 1995, one of the first national real estate companies to do so. The company initially underestimated the complexity of its foray into cyberspace. Web site development requires significant technical support and extensive research and planning, a lesson that Coldwell Banker learned the hard way.

Underappreciated by the company's brokers and underused by potential customers, the site struggled through its first year. The roots of the problems were that the company hadn't cultivated broker buy-in, and site functionality and support were inadequate.

There was no doubt about it: Coldwell Banker's site needed revamping. Regina Taylor, Coldwell Banker senior vice president of marketing, reevaluated the effort and determined what was required to capture the choice advantage. As Taylor confides: "We quickly realized we had to invest a lot more into the site than the company had originally anticipated. To transform it into a successful and integral part of the company's business, we determined that there were four areas we needed to focus on. We had to have an efficient means of data collection to get the listings from all of our offices. We had to skillfully communicate to our brokers the company's aims for the site and its use. We had to provide excellent customer service to our franchisees; we were asking them to give us all their listing information in a short period of time, so we had to make this job as easy as possible for them. And finally, we had to concentrate on great site functionality. If the site wasn't comprehensive, robust, user-friendly, and valuable, then nobody would use it. Site functionality is of utmost importance—attractive design that's hard to use is a waste of money."

The company hired Interealty, one of the nation's largest multiple listing service (MLS) companies, to redesign the site. "We were taking something of a risk," explains Taylor, "as Interealty was not a traditional site design company. However, we knew that they understood the real estate business and the importance of connecting with our brokers and personalizing our relationship with customers."

By late 1996, the company had implemented a number of strategic changes and the improved site made its debut on February 3, 1997. Today, visitors to Coldwell Banker Online can view more than 200,000 properties with an aggregate value of more than $35 billion. It's all there: photos, square footage, floor plans, architectural details, special features and amenities like that whirlpool tub no one can live without, and details about the neighborhood including shopping and schools.

Visitors to Coldwell Banker Online first enter the so-called property search area, which asks them to specify the location, size, price, and type of property they are looking for. Specialized listings include luxury homes, resort properties, new homes, military market housing, and university area housing. A similar search service also exists for commercial properties.

Launched on January 19, 1998, the Personal Retriever (PR) service makes things even easier. It asks for name, address (optional), e-mail address, and desired specifications. The customer can then sign off and go about her life, while Personal Retriever does the work. Within hours, she gets an e-mail detailing properties that meet her criteria. Also included are current interest rates from various lenders. When a new listing becomes available, Personal Retriever sends it right along. The service also updates interest rate information—a real plus for customers waiting for rates to go down. And to help customers determine what they could get for their homes, Personal Retriever lists the prices on comparable houses that have recently sold in their neighborhood.

Customers choose how often they want Personal Retriever to notify them—daily, weekly, or monthly—and with what information. Each customer is entitled to five active searches. Thus, a customer can request information, say, on all one-bedroom apartments under $350,000 in midtown Manhattan, as well as all three-bedroom vacation homes for under $500,000 on Cape Cod—and still have three searches left. A Montana ranch, anyone?

For potential buyers of its luxury Previews properties, the site offers virtual house tours. Using IPIX 360-degree technology, the well-heeled glide from room to room—and if that inlaid marble mantle catches their fancy they can zoom right in on it. The service requires the customer to download (for free) more advanced software, but that's a small price to pay for the privilege of previewing multimillion-dollar digs.

Wonder what your new neighborhood will be like? Click into Neighborhood Explorer and learn about the school system, climate, housing prices, and demographics. Information Booth allows visitors to check current financing rates, and use such services as a mortgage calculator and a home price comparison index. Also, on every listing or agent profile page, an access button enables the visitor to contact a local Coldwell Banker office.

The rate of conversion from visitor to customer stands at about 1 percent. But the company expects that number to rise as they hone their offering through services such as Personal Retriever. It costs Coldwell Banker significantly less to generate leads from its Web site than it does from traditional advertising.

Because of the dynamic and unique nature of its inventory, Coldwell Banker strives to ensure that its Web site includes nearly 100 percent of its listings. This requires a significant amount of site support because thousands of listings come on and off each day. The company's brokers—who are more comfortable with the site since its relaunch and are seeing concrete results—have become diligent partners in keeping information up to date.

An unanticipated benefit of the Web site is an enhanced relationship between agent and customer. Since customers are more knowledgeable about their choices and there is less time spent visiting homes that are simply all wrong, the agent can focus on securing the best financing and closing the sale.

The company sees the site as an addition to its sales force and not a replacement. Home buying is a complex transaction and the most expensive purchase most people make in their lifetimes—an agent plays an irreplaceable role. The site also works in other profitable ways for Coldwell Banker. It helps attract new franchises and assists brokers in recruiting and retaining sales associates.

Currently Coldwell Banker's Web site receives between six million and ten million hits per week. Coldwell Banker is striving to make sure that visitors are greeted by a friendly site that details their choices in a helpful manner—and works with them to turn the complex process of home buying into a rewarding experience.

❏ *How Coldwell Banker clicks with choice:*

1. By creating buy-in across the entire company.
2. By creating interactive search engines that narrow choices.
3. By inviting visitors to explore the many choices available to them in an easy and convenient way.
4. By creating a site that understands and addresses the emotional component of home ownership, offering information on "peripherals" like neighborhoods, schools, and shops.
5. By positioning the Web site so it would complement, rather than replace, employees.
6. By partnering with a company that understands both the complexities of technology and the intricacies of the choices customers must make.

How You Can Click with Choice

- By being clear. When customers face complex options, savvy businesses—like Coldwell Banker and Marshall Industries—provide explanations written in plain English readily available on online, thereby increasing the likelihood of sales. You should, too.
- By building a database of customer preferences using a history of purchases and a voluntary questionnaire. Coldwell Banker uses sophisticated information technology that automatically e-mails customers about offerings they may find interesting or that match their recorded preferences.

- By making the most of chat rooms. They provide opportunities for customers to share their opinions with each other. These first-person testimonials often carry more weight than official company advertising pronouncements. Also, chat rooms build loyalty and strengthen customers' emotional ties to your organization.

- By making it easy for customers to search your inventory of products or services. Your bottom line will be the better for it. Without the assistance of a capable search engine, your customers are likely to feel overwhelmed and flee.

- By stocking the items you sell online. Why? Customers are disappointed when they have to wait weeks or months for an item. Also, provide up-to-the-minute information on the item's availability, and the status of a particular order.

- By keeping the store open. Even a successful Web site can benefit from a physical store. Some online customers may be letting their fingers do the typing only to see what range of choices they have, then making the actual purchases in person. This is particularly true for high-ticket items like cars, boats, and electronics. Few people plunk down $10,000 for a state-of-the-art home entertainment center without checking out the picture and sound quality in person. In short, Web sites don't replace physical stores. Rather, they can improve sales both online and on site.

4

Click with Convenience

Make it convenient for your customer.
Make it efficient for yourself.

W hat is the convenience advantage?

A century ago, the apothecary, haberdashery, and general store had the convenience advantage if you could walk to them in ten minutes. Later, they had the convenience advantage if you could drive to them in ten minutes. Now you can't even reach some of the best emporiums by jet plane.

They're out there in cyberspace, wherever that is, yet paradoxically they are far closer than a ten-minute walk. With a few clicks of your index finger, you can levitate yourself right through your favorite merchant's front door.

Convenience? Thanks to the Web, time and space are disappearing, along with inconvenience, an artifact of a mode of commerce that companies that do business on the Internet aim to obliterate.

Who has the convenience advantage?

In this chapter, we profile four Web-wise companies that sell convenience to customers both outside and inside their organizations.

Peapod, Inc., pioneered online grocery shopping. Here, we show how it designed its site to provide a remarkable range of customer options.

Federal Express Corporation (a subsidiary of FDX Corporation) brought convenience to the overnight-delivery industry that it also invented. Like Peapod, it has harnessed its Web site to benefit customers in ways never glimpsed before. The site enables Asian, European, North American, and South American customers to prepare and print airbills and shipping documentation, receive online delivery information for incoming packages, and orchestrate advance customs clearances. Beyond all that, it allows corporate customers to achieve unprecedented integration with their suppliers as well as their end users.

Pitney Bowes, Inc. has found ways to organize its dozens of products online to provide the greatest possible customer convenience.

And 1-800-Flowers, Inc., having blossomed selling flowers by phone, has found the Internet an even better way of selling its core service—convenience. How committed is this company to perfecting itself as a clickable corporation? In its first three Web years, 1-800-Flowers redesigned its site completely five times, gaining experience so invaluable that reading about it in this chapter could save substantial time and money for any company assessing a move to the Internet.

Peapod Clicks with Convenience

Let your fingers do the walking and your mouse do the shopping. With a few clicks you can buy all your groceries and have them delivered right to your home. Welcome to Peapod (www.peapod.com) and the world of online grocery shopping—where the advantage is 100 percent convenience.

Peapod, Inc. was founded in 1989 on the premise that advanced technology could make online grocery shopping convenient and affordable for shoppers—and profitable for grocers. Co-founders Andrew Parkinson and his brother Thomas—the company's chief executive officer and chief technology officer respectively—have applied their vision with diligence and imagination. The result has been an Internet supermarket that saves customers time, energy, and aggravation.

How does Peapod deliver on its promise? By allowing customers to perform a traditionally laborious task quickly and easily. Offering more than 25,000 different items, the site employs certified professional shoppers, who hand-pick each order. The produce specialists choose only the best fruits and vegetables according to Produce Marketing Association standards. Each order stays fresh (or frozen) thanks to temperature controlled delivery containers and reaches the customer in better shape than if she had shopped herself.

Watching those fat grams or searching for high-calcium vegetables? With a click, you can read FDA nutritional information or sort food by fat, cholesterol, or sodium content. Shoppers are also promised they will "never create a shopping list from scratch again"—Peapod's keeps a customer's last five orders on file and items can be automatically selected. No more forgetting the milk.

Shopping can be done twenty-four hours a day, 365 days a year, and same- or next-day delivery to a customer's home or office is available seven days a week. Technical support and member care specialists are available online at all times. And worries about weather, traffic, parking, or lugging grocery bags are simply nonexistent. Peapod's friendly service people deliver each order perfectly—guaranteed.

Peapod's first foray into cyberspace was a private computer network for ordering groceries online. In a small Chicago-area test run, the system proved extremely popular despite the fact that it was built on a private on-line service and required expensive (for Peapod) toll-free lines. The network was also limited in size and speed.

Then along came the Internet, and Peapod wasted no time in seizing the convenience advantage. The company shut down its costly private network, radically expanded its capabilities, and in 1994 officially launched Internet service. The subsequent development of its site has focused on offering faster service and easier access. As Andrew Parkinson explains, a key challenge was the size of an average grocery order. "We quickly realized that the technology for our site had to be much faster and more functional than other sites conducting Internet commerce. There's a big difference between buying a book or two online and buying 55 grocery items, which is our average order. The keys to e-commerce are what you are selling and how you are selling it. Both have to work in tandem for the customer."

With an eye to customer feedback, Peapod developed and implemented a new generation of software in early 1998. The main features are accelerated speed, the ability to access other Web pages while shopping, and a visual representation for every purchase. The online shopping cart actually fills up with jars of peanut butter and stalks of celery, avoiding the hazard of forgetting what you've already bought and being surprised when the delivery man arrives with six jars of Jiffy.

Peapod's success is reflected in its growth. Since 1994, it has expanded from its Chicago base to serve San Francisco, Columbus, Boston,

Houston, Dallas, and Austin—and has plans to enter a number of other metropolitan markets.

The Peapod Web site is dominated by bold green print, bright graphics, and simple instructions. After logging on, new customers receive instructions that guide them through the short process of downloading Peapod software and securing their passwords. They now have the keys to the store. The site offers a number of organizational schemes. Virtual shoppers find groceries separated into categories such as produce, dairy, meats, and canned goods. Alternatively, a customer can search for a general item such as canned corn, or a particular brand such as Green Giant. Or shoppers can base their choices on calorie count, fat content, or price. Making these kinds of comparisons in an actual store takes a lot of time and effort—with Peapod it's done in a click.

Addicted to coupons? No problem. Peapod points its customers toward both its own and manufacturers' savings and special promotions. The result is the kind of impulse buys that all merchants love.

The "past shopping list" feature is a real convenience. Each time a member visits the site, a list of his or her last five shopping orders appears and items can be added or deleted as desired. This eliminates the need to browse electronic aisles for regularly bought items. Gone are the days of arriving at the meat counter only to realize you forgot the eggs seven aisles back. Customers choose the day and time they want their groceries delivered and Peapod strives to get there within a ninety-minute window.

Convenience doesn't come free. Peapod customers pay a membership fee, a flat shopping and delivery fee, and a surcharge based on the amount of the total bill. The company is currently experimenting with different combinations of these fees as it tries to find ways of lowering its prices. According to a recent study, consumer interest in shopping online rises dramatically as the cost falls. Only 4 percent of those surveyed expressed an interest when a fee of $15 was quoted. This number increased to 18 percent when a fee of between $10 and $15 was named, and rose as high as 77 percent when the charge dropped below $10.

The demographics of Peapod members are revealing; the company is tapping into a lucrative market that prizes convenience. Eighty percent of its members work, the large majority of them full-time, and almost half of them have annual household incomes in excess of $100,000. Interestingly, 80 percent of Peapod's members are female. Considering that male Internet users still outnumber female,* the company has obviously won over a hard-to-reach audience.

Since customer convenience is always its primary objective, Peapod takes advantage of every opportunity to solicit feedback. Random surveys are conducted on a regular basis, as are focus groups to gauge reaction to new concepts. The company employs usability testing to judge both its own software and that of its competitors.

These efforts have produced visible results. The site's ability to "maintain state" (techno-speak for staying connected to the user during the buying process) gives it a definite advantage over its competitors. Every time you make a purchase at other online stores, the screen is likely to disappear for a few seconds as the software registers the buy. Peapod keeps the customer moving swiftly, easily, and without interruption.

Parkinson says, "We are always sensitive not to get in the way of the consumer. Our customers use us for convenience; in no way do we want

*Colin Shaddick, "Internet Advertising Poised to Change Buyers' Habits," *Marketing Week*, January 15, 1998, pp. 32–33.

to jeopardize that by slowing them down, either through forced advertising or slow technology. In order to build loyalty, everything you do has to bring value to the customer."

From 1996 to 1997, Peapod's enrollment more than doubled to 71,500 members, four out of five of whom are expected to remain loyal customers. During these two years, the company's revenues also more than doubled to almost $60 million. Predictions for growth of the overall online grocery market are also impressive, with some experts estimating it will account for more than 20 percent of total grocery volume by the year 2003. That translates into an $80 billion industry.

As the pioneer in this market, Peapod has made some mistakes; however, as Parkinson suggests, these are to be expected. "Most of this business is not invented as of yet. Everything is basically developed as you go, through listening to the customer and from continual improvement."

The company, for instance, is currently reorienting its relationship with grocery store chains such as Stop-n-Shop and the Jewel Stores. Previously Peapod filled customer orders through these chains. Although this strategy helped reduce some of Peapod's overhead costs, it tied the company to the stores' inventory levels. One solution has been warehouses owned in partnership with the stores.

Hand-held scanners have also helped reduce costs and increase the quality of Peapod's service. Using these scanners, clerks who fill customers' orders automatically send a reorder message to the inventory database. The technology also allows the clerk to complete a "checkout" by simply pressing a button.

Peapod's goals center on streamlining its operations and expanding into additional markets. The company is a true Web pioneer, harnessing new technology to capture the convenience advantage.

❏ *How Peapod clicks with convenience:*

1. By emphasizing speed, simplicity, and consistency.

2. By tracking the details of repeated transactions.

3. By watching logistics—ensuring that products are in stock, delivered on time, and guaranteed to be of high quality.

FedEx Clicks with Convenience

In 1973, when Federal Express (www.fedex.com) opened its van and cargo-bay doors for business, the words "overnight delivery" conjured up images of either luxury or emergency. Today, sending things overnight is a fact of everyday life. The change is due in large part to the standards set by FedEx for fast, reliable, and—most important—convenient service.

FedEx—one of the great business success stories of the last fifty years—operates a door-to-door, customs-cleared network that guarantees global delivery within twenty-four to forty-eight hours. Its 600 aircraft and 40,000 vehicles move three million items to 211 countries every working day. In 1998, revenues reached $13.3 billion. None of this happened by accident—it was the result of brilliant business minds boldly leveraging emerging technologies.

In 1985 FedEx introduced PowerShip, a revolutionary hardware/software system that enables customers to manage transactions from their computers. They can ship goods, print airbills, receive billing information, request courier pickup, and track the status of packages as they travel across the globe. As FedEx's executive vice president and chief financial officer Alan Graf explains, "We've pioneered the use of information to get closer to customers and give them better and quicker information for their own use with our PowerShip program."

From day one, the company has maintained a fierce focus on convenience. That focus is still sharp and, as Graf says, it's the reason the Web site attracts "close to ten million hits per month. We know that over two million packages are tracked each month, and that number is growing. Our customers have full control of their packages by accessing our database. They don't have to call a FedEx customer service center and tie up a customer service agent to do that tracking and tracing. So it's a win-win for both us and our customers."

FedEx continues to expand its repertoire of Internet functions. The site includes a feature called interNetShip that allows customers worldwide to print airbills and shipping documentation as well as receive online delivery information for incoming packages. Then there's NetReturn, which handles product returns. Merchants simply enter the relevant information and FedEx electronically arranges for pickup, labeling, tracking, and delivery—just as with outbound packages. For many of its business customers, FedEx has become a fully integrated corporate partner, one that picks up, transports, warehouses, and delivers goods from factory to receiving dock—with status data available every step of the way.

Some large companies have handed over their entire logistics management to FedEx. Today, products manufactured by National Semiconductor's six Asian factories are shipped directly to a FedEx distribution warehouse in Singapore. In essence, National Semiconductor uses FedEx as its distributor and enjoys convenience as well as cost savings.

By integrating its private information network with its public Internet presence, FedEx has developed an information-systems model—called "network convergence"—that is fast becoming a global standard.

In a celebrated example, FedEx played a major role in pharmaceutical giant Pfizer's launch of Viagra, the drug for enhancing male sexual performance. As Graf explains, Pfizer "wanted everything to arrive at the pharmacists at the very moment the company announced the launch. We did that through their warehouses and the FedEx distribution network, and were able to do it cost-effectively because we have their electronic database in our network and they have ours in theirs."

FedEx spends $1 billion a year developing, implementing, and maintaining its information technology—nearly 10 percent of its annual revenues. It may seem like a large price to pay for convenience, but not when it's the company's core value proposition. Indeed, the rapid expansion of Internet technology promises even deeper integration of information systems between FedEx and its customers.

❏ *How FedEx clicks with convenience:*

1. By putting customers in control of their transactions.
2. By integrating its systems with those of its customers.
3. By going beyond package delivery into full-fledged, Web-based partnerships with customers.
4. By developing networks with sophisticated time- and labor-saving capabilities.

Pitney Bowes Clicks with Convenience

In today's wired world it's easy to imagine "snail mail"—a.k.a. regular postal services—slipping into extinction as surely as the dodo bird. But don't write the eulogies just yet. Venerable Pitney Bowes (www.pb.com), a long-time leader in postage metering and mail-handling products, is proving that a company doesn't have to be the new kid on the block to know how to capitalize on the latest technology.

This seventy-five-year-old company has a long history of redefining itself to take advantage of technological advances. Today, that means the Internet—and Pitney Bowes is right there. As executive director of external affairs Sheryl Battles says, "You have a vast range of applications available today, and depending on what you're doing, you may need faxing, e-mail, or Internet solutions. The point is that you have to have available several convenient forms for communicating."

The company has come a long way from the mechanical device that brought it to prominence. The nation's first stamp had been issued in 1847, but it was Arthur Pitney's invention of the postage meter at the turn of the century—and his alliance with industrialist Walter Bowes in 1920—that enabled businesses to save time and money by printing postage directly onto their mail. Today, the metered mail industry is a multibillion-dollar business dominated by Pitney Bowes.

Since those early days, Pitney Bowes has used technological advances to expand its business, which today is centered on helping companies manage the movement of all types of messages, documents, and packages. Its products range from compact postage meters cost-effective enough to work for small businesses, to software that lets large mail centers embed customer information in mailing data, to advanced faxing and copying solutions, to serving as a document manager for the commercial and legal industries.

In a very real sense, Pitney Bowes is dependent on the United States Postal Service. Only the USPS can legally authorize products that issue stamps or print evidence of postage paid. Thus Pitney Bowes is seeking

USPS approval for technology that can turn a PC and a printer into a desktop mailroom. This represents a real breakthrough capable of saving time, effort, energy, and above all, money. No more standing in lines at the post office or self-service kiosks to buy stamps; no more searching through cluttered desks to find the dispenser. All a Pitney Bowes customer would have to do is go online.

In addition to the PC-stamp, the company is developing a suite of products that support the pre-and post-stamping process. This includes software that supports the distribution of mail upon its arrival at a location. For Pitney Bowes, the idea is to create a virtual mailroom, postage meter, or messaging system—and tie them all together into a single online communications system that will provide new levels of convenience for customers.

In preparation for those developments, Pitney Bowes launched its Internet Web site in 1996. The site serves as an interactive vehicle for customer communications and as a catalog for selling an ever-expanding range of products. Each of the company's divisions designed its own portion of the site. "The divisions have different sites because the customer bases are different," says the marketing manager of the supplies division, Susan Garvey, "and therefore the use of the Internet for that customer base is different."

The site is a highly focused, custom-tailored marketing interface. From its original twenty-two products, customer demand quickly prompted Pitney Bowes to offer its full fifty-six-page catalog. Everything Pitney Bowes sells over the Internet is available at a 10-percent discount. This reduction is made possible because online transactions cost the company less than telephone orders.

Pitney Bowes's Small Office division is using advertising—direct response, television, and print—to drive traffic to its Web site. As a result, a large proportion of new customers—mostly midsized and smaller businesses—are ordering online. According to Beth Ghiloni, marketing manager for the Small Office division, the Internet "is my fourth largest distribution channel after telemarketing, direct mail, and direct response to television—and it's growing all the time."

The company's managers are finding that the entire site is a locus of cross-selling and value-added marketing. Customers may enter the Small Office site and then move to the Supplies site to order core products. The sales force, seeking to generate leads, can easily identify the right person to contact at a company. This is an example of internal convenience generated by Internet know-how.

Pitney Bowes can manage—either on or off a customer's premises—all mailing, copying, and document production, electronic printing, records management, and electronic imaging. In time, the company believes, the Internet will assume many of these functions. This will be an enormous convenience for customers, who will be free to focus on core business issues.

True to its techno-savvy traditions, Pitney Bowes intends to leverage the power of the Internet to remain the leader in providing communications solutions to companies large and small.

❑ *How Pitney Bowes clicks with convenience:*

1. By creating a multifunctional Web site that allows customers to move seamlessly from one area to another.
2. By streamlining the work of its marketing staff through Internet-related leads and cross-selling.

3. By building a virtual mailroom that handles customers' internal and external communication, freeing them to focus on the core business.

1-800-Flowers Clicks with Convenience

We've all been there. Going about our day without a care, we glance at the calendar and discover to our horror that it's our parents' anniversary, our spouse's birthday, or a best friend's first day on a new job. Giftless and with no time to spare, we frantically seek a solution.

Since 1984, 1-800-FLOWERS (www.1800flowers.com) has been helping folks out of these and other tight squeezes. With just a phone call—or a trip to the Internet—you can order same-day delivery of the perfect bouquet, gift basket, plant, or balloon arrangement. Having built strong brand recognition and a product that is well suited to the needs of the Internet user, 1-800-FLOWERS is making a profit online by stressing customer convenience as its main selling theme.

Originally based in Dallas, the company was purchased by New York City florist Jim McCann in 1987. McCann's strategy has been simple: Promote flowers as gifts and make ordering them as convenient as possible. In essence, according to the company's vice president of interactive services, Donna Iucolano, McCann wanted his organization to become the L. L. Bean of florists—offering excellent customer service with absolute quality guarantees and rapid order fulfillment. McCann has opened 150 franchise-owned stores where customers can buy flowers in person, but the core of the business is still phone-based orders distributed worldwide through the 2,500 partner florists of the company's "BloomNet."

Always looking for new and innovative marketing methods, 1-800-

FLOWERS began advertising on the fledging Cable News Network (CNN) in the late 1980s. During the 1991 Persian Gulf War, McCann took advantage of the hesitancy some companies had to advertise during wartime and snatched up all the air time he could at greatly reduced prices. The result was a bonanza of publicity and a big step toward becoming, as the company proclaims itself, "the world's largest florist."

An interactive division was formed during the winter of 1992. According to chief operating officer Chris McCann, Jim's brother, "the electronic medium was profitable for us basically from day one." Still, Internet sales were accounting for only $150,000 in annual revenue until the company established a presence on AOL, which launched in November 1994. And in April 1995, 1-800-FLOWERS launched its own Web site.

"Our efforts were transactional from day one, and our product was in perfect synergy with who was online in those days," says Iucolano. "It was primarily men [95 percent] who were well-employed, well-educated, very technologically savvy, and often in trouble for spending too much time away from their families. We had an inexpensive product that would solve their problem, and it was something they didn't have to try on or even think much about. They could just send an order in, twenty-four hours a day, seven days a week."

In 1996, thanks in large part to strong customer bonding and the convenience with which it delivered on its value proposition, 1-800-FLOWERS had more transactions on its Web site than any other company in the United States. By mid-1998 over $30 million—more than 10 percent of the company's annual revenue—had been generated online. In 1997 the company paid AOL $25 million for the right to remain its exclusive florist—a deal expected to bring in $250 million in sales by 2001. There are also partnerships with more than 100 other online businesses.

One of the keys to the success of 1-800-FLOWERS has been its ability to offer superb service on its busiest days—Mother's Day, Valentine's Day, and Easter—by gearing up with extra employees, inventory, and resources. In addition, Internet customers can set up a free "reminder service"—the company will e-mail them notices of birthdays, anniversaries, and holidays. The service not only provides low-cost marketing for the company, it has no doubt saved more than one marriage.

The customer who shops online can view the floral assortments, gift baskets, and other offerings before they put them in a virtual shopping cart. Credit card authorization is conducted in real time, and all orders made by 3:00 P.M. are guaranteed for same-day delivery.

Both Iucolano and Chris McCann believe that 1-800-FLOWERS has made such a smooth transition to the Internet because it already had a strong infrastructure in place. Being a phone-order-based company, it was experienced in handling such issues as order tracking, product fulfillment, and rapid, secure credit card authorization. These same problems stall many companies moving online, but as Iucolano explains, "Our Internet start-up costs and development time were much lower because of our experiences with the telecenter side of our business. We knew how to handle rapid product fulfillment and deal with order buildup during holidays. We had relationships developed with the credit card companies and had dealt with problems of security. We could concentrate more on sales and marketing from the start because we had the hard part of the business in place."

Customers can use the site as an electronic catalog, then actually place orders by telephone. The sales conversion rate on these "look-first" calls is nearly 100 percent, and calls tend to be shorter. Telephone reps are able to close transactions faster than they can on strictly telephone orders. Then there are customers who order through the site but call with service questions; still others order by phone but e-mail questions to the company.

The company is committed to continual enhancement of its site, which went through five functional and graphic redesigns during its first three years. In order to keep costs down during these revamps, it acts as a test partner for companies developing new e-commerce products and services—and receives these advances at a steep discount. This translates into cutting-edge technology at a major savings.

The company uses the Internet to aggressively solicit customer feedback. It e-mails some twenty-five regular customers each time it plans a site redesign. Giving these customers a private URL address, the company asked them to take a "sneak peek" and comment. Customers have suggested user-friendly improvements such as a "one-click" capability to return to the home page.

All of these measures mean an increase in quality—and revenue—for the 1-800-FLOWERS site. "Our business has been growing by more than 100 percent every year," says Iucolano. Comparing the site to its traditional phone-based sales model, she points to the fact the company can reach a global audience on the Internet without the problems of different time zones and long-distance phone charges. The company passes these savings on to its customers in the form of a lower—by $3.00—service charge on Web site orders.

To get more of its business to move online, 1-800-FLOWERS has its telephone representatives ask customers for their e-mail addresses. To the approximately 20 percent who comply, the company e-mails their telephone order confirmations—establishing an electronic dialog. "What we're finding," says Chris McCann, "is that many of these people we e-mail for the first time send us back an e-mail saying how impressed they are to get an electronic message. Then they e-mail us again to say how much their Aunt Rose liked the flowers. So now we've established a channel for them to have an ongoing dialog with us, which holds tremendous potential."

Internet dialog also helps 1-800-FLOWERS keep in touch with its BloomNet partners. In addition to making sure orders and messages are transmitted properly, the company can provide information on which crops are coming up at different farms in the 48 countries the company imports from. "In a way," says McCann, "we're building a virtual community for our flower shops—our internal customers—that provide the service to our external customers."

McCann predicts that by the year 2000 the Web site will account for up to 15 percent of total revenue and will expand to reach a greater diversity of consumers. Brand trust established over time is a major factor that brings customers to 1-800-FLOWERS, but by making its site as convenient as possible—for both the customer and itself—the company has captured an advantage that will keep people coming back.

❏ *How 1-800-Flowers clicks with convenience:*

1. By offering a quick and painless solution to a common problem.
2. By delivering same day through its BloomNet.

3. By creating a site where customers can actually see the products before they buy.
4. By enhancing communication with its suppliers.
5. By testing cutting-edge Internet technology and receiving a discount on its use.

How You Can Click with Convenience

- By making a long and laborious task quick and easy. A company that takes a time-consuming chore online and makes it convenient and user-friendly—such as Peapod does with grocery shopping—will win grateful customers.
- By keeping track of your products and services twenty-four hours a day, anywhere on the globe. Enabling customers to check on the status of their purchases, as FedEx does, adds value for both buyer and seller. Customers are put at ease, and the company is able to more effectively manage its resources and inventory management.
- By performing tasks that customers don't want to do. Pitney Bowes uses the Internet to take over routine office processes and free customers to focus on their core strengths. You can, too.
- By integrating other sales capabilities with your Internet offering. Use your Web site as an online catalog, but allow customers the convenience of making a purchase either online or through another medium, such as mail or telephone.
- By using e-mail to establish a dialog with customers—solicit their ideas, find out what annoys them or wastes their time. 1-800-Flowers enjoys a lively e-relationship with its customers, and it has been able

to provide innovative conveniences like gift lists that make sure your favorite aunt automatically gets her lily at Easter. "Remind" customers when they are about to run out of an item or when important dates are approaching.

- By using state-of-the-art technology. Such capabilities as 1-800-Flowers' reminder service require sophisticated technology to handle all the variables—customers' previous orders, preferences, seasonal gifts, special occasions, and so on. If your site offers convenience, it must be powered by an adequate technology and be engineered to handle peak usage. It serves no purpose to cut corners here.

5

Click with Customization

Customize your product.
Personalize your approach.

In the movie *Field of Dreams,* Kevin Costner plays a baseball-loving farmer, who hears a disembodied voice instructing him to build a big ballpark in the middle of his Iowa cornfield. "If you build it, they will come," the voice repeats.

This might well be the mantra of traditional businesses as they pursue the customization advantage. When it comes to pursuing this advantage on the Internet, we would like to suggest a variation: "Let them build it, and they will come."

Who has the customization advantage?

Ask them to come online, and then let them build the product they ask for. That is the inspired strategy of two technology powerhouses, Dell

Computer Corporation and Cisco Systems, Inc. In this chapter, we see how they captured the customization advantage.

By no coincidence, these two companies are the Internet's top money-makers, according to the April 1998 Cowles/Simba survey. Dell Computer (number two) enables online customers to select components and tell the company's technicians how they want them assembled. At Dell, in short, the user rules. The customization advantage is largely responsible for its estimated online revenue, which in 1998 exceeded $2 billion annually.

Cisco Systems (number one) is the worldwide leader in networking for the Internet. In 1998, the company rang up online sales of more than $4.5 billion. In terms of overall revenue from the Internet, Cisco Systems owns by far the most successful Web site on earth.

Let's take a look at both.

Dell Clicks with Customization

With 1998 revenues of $15.2 billion and a 9 percent market share, Dell Computer Corporation (www.dell.com) is the world's second largest computer manufacturer. The company sells directly to large and small businesses, government agencies, academic institutions, and individuals. In 1998, Dell's sales increased 59 percent and profits zoomed 82 percent.

The company's success secrets? Direct relationships with customers, savvy management of inventory, and high-quality products customized to fit any customer's needs. In a move of breathtaking simplicity and brilliance, Dell sells directly to customers—offering them the opportunity to design their own computers, adding whatever capabilities, bells, and whistles they desire. Dell acquires the components from its suppliers on an as-needed basis, eliminating the expense of middlemen—and keeping prices competitive. When Intel issues a new Pentium processor, for example, Dell isn't caught holding a large inventory of suddenly outdated models. And Dell's customized computers are high-quality machines, backed by service and parts guarantees. That's the basic value proposition that's made the company one of the most successful in recent business history.

The telephone has been Dell's lifeline since its founding in 1984. Sensing new worlds of opportunity in online commerce, managers turned their attention to the question of how the Internet could enhance their direct-sales approach. The company conducted a survey of both regular customers and casual visitors to its Web site, which it first created in 1996. The question? What do you want most? The answer? Fast, accurate, and effective technical support. This became the Web site's mission.

Dell set to work expanding its already substantial database of technical-support information—and deploying it onto the Web site. If customers had a problem getting their computers to recognize a hard drive or to connect with a modem, they could type in a brief description of the problem, identify the components they were using, and instantaneously view Dell's problem-solving manual.

According to Scott Eckert, director of online services, Dell's Internet commerce relies on three qualities:

1. An information-technology system that speaks the customer's language. Every company develops its own internal shorthand—key words and phrases that grow out of its culture and operation and that are understood by all employees. For any company—but especially a high-tech, direct-sales company like Dell—this can be a problem. Even the most dedicated computerphiles can have trouble grasping rapid-fire internal Dellspeak. And so the company constructed an information-technology

system geared to the customer rather than the company's products and functions. The language is user friendly, and applications are doable even for novices.

2. Internet commerce that is fully integrated with business processes. Without seamless communication between all functions, Dell wouldn't be able to deliver what customers want: the ability to retrieve information, shop, build a new hardware system, complete an order quickly, have it processed accurately, and receive the product in good working order. "All of these things," Eckert says,"must be fully integrated with your information systems so that the whole process is as easy and pleasant for the customer as it would be if he or she called on the telephone and talked to a sales representative."

3. Online support capability that can help customers solve their own problems. A Dell owner can customize his or her own solution to a problem. Online diagnostic flowcharts take the customer step by step through the same processes that Dell's technicians follow. A file library provides updated drivers that the customer can download to help get a system back up and running smoothly.

Dell's target Internet audience is sophisticated "Web savvy" individuals who have done their homework before they contact the site. They know what the competition offers; they've read the consumer advice columns and know that they want a 400MHz processor, a 56K modem, and 64MB of RAM. Thus, when they sign on, they're primed to select from a wide variety of components, add-on features, and peripherals. And with a quick click they can find out the price. If it busts their budget, options are presented for lowering it—for instance, by selecting the next best monitor or speaker system. Likewise, they can upgrade if they come in under budget or feel like splurging.

Once the customer is satisfied with the design, he or she completes the sale with a credit card. Dell's astute management of its supply chain means that the order is processed and filled within a few days—and the computer is on its way to its home anywhere around the world.

Some Internet shoppers use the site primarily to gather data, check on prices, and compare machines, but then prefer to work with a sales representative to make the actual purchase. For this kind of customer the Web site functions as a support service and/or an introduction to the company, not as a revenue generator in its own right. Without the Web site, however, many of those customers would never have come to the company in the first place. It allows them to explore their options without the pressure of talking to a phone representative. This is especially valuable for first-time users who may feel inhibited asking basic questions or tying up an operator for a long period of time. When they finally do take the plunge, however, Dell has found that novice buyers like the reassurance of human contact. Computers are a big-ticket item and buying one electronically still makes many consumers uneasy.

For many veteran computer buyers, however, online customization and direct purchase have become second nature. For some seven thousand of its largest corporate clients, Dell offers a feature called Premier Pages, where—with a click—the company can review its entire ordering history, the prices it has paid, technical support it has received, its credit and purchasing arrangements, in fact every contact it has had with Dell. And, of course, it can make an order. Premier Pages is another reflection of Dell's commitment to customization at every level and in every function, not just the building of computers.

Eckert attributes Dell's Internet success to "working directly with customers, understanding their needs, and building a distribution network model around those needs. This is a high-velocity, low-cost distribution mechanism for some very good products, and above all it is a highly customized customer experience."

Dell's Web site currently has annual sales exceeding $2 billion a year, a little more than 10 percent of the company's overall total. Fully 40 percent of the people buying online are individual consumers, who as a group account for about 10 percent of Dell customers. The company is working to increase online sales to 50 percent of total sales, and for the ratio of business-to-individual customers to eventually match its overall ratio.

Replacing the paper-based workflow with electronic processes may not happen overnight, but Dell has an advantage over its Internet competitors. IBM, Hewlett-Packard, and Compaq all offer their products through retailers, many of whom are threatened by Internet selling. These companies, therefore, need to consider offering their retailers incentives such as lower wholesale prices—but if they do so, they reduce their own revenues. Dell has been built from day one on direct selling, and so it has experience and know-how that is a natural match for the Web.

Dell Online is proving that the Internet doesn't necessarily depersonalize customer relationships; rather, it has the potential to enhance them. The Web site has strengthened the company's commitment to dealing directly with its customers—on their own time, at their own pace. Dell wants its customers to be educated about their choices, to understand what they need in a computer—and what they *don't* need. It wants to work with customers to build them their perfect computer—one that fits their budget, their life, even their decor. It's called customization and Dell is using the Internet to take it to new heights.

❏ *How Dell clicks with customization:*

1. By educating customers as to their choices and then working with them to build a computer that perfectly fits their needs.
2. By creating Premier Pages—a customized, detailed summary of all transactions—for its corporate customers.
3. By providing step-by-step online technical support that enables customers to customize solutions to their problems.

Cisco Systems Clicks with Customization

Cisco Systems (www.cisco.com), a provider of sophisticated computer hardware, software, and expertise is transforming the way companies and whole industries do business. For Cisco, the Internet isn't just a catalog or an order book, it's a means for the company to integrate its entire operation—and those of its suppliers and customers.

With competitors such as Lucent Technologies, Inc., and Nortel Telecom, Ltd. still a long way behind, Cisco is shaping the way companies integrate internally, with their customers, and with other businesses. The company works with large organizations that have their own complex networks, with Internet service providers (ISPs), and with small and medium-sized businesses that need data networks or need to connect to the Internet. By making such interactions efficient and cost effective, chiefly by customizing them for each client, Cisco has become a trailblazer through the wilds of Cyberspace.

"In the five years I've been here, we've grown from a $400 million company to an $8 billion company," explains Peter Solvik, chief information officer of Cisco Systems. "We've done it without building factories or hiring hundreds of assembly people. Moving online was the major step we needed to increase our power."

Cisco is often referred to as the "plumber" of the Internet: It supplies the fittings and valves needed to make network connections, and the faucets and fixtures that enable those networks to link in Cyberspace. It's a truism that if you control travel routes—sea lanes, highways, and skies—you control the entire landscape. And in the digital age, there is no more important travel route than the Internet. By dominating the Internet building-block market, Cisco shows signs of being the ultimate master of its domain.

Cisco was founded in 1984, built on one product—the multiprotocol router—developed by two Stanford University professors, Leonard Bosack and Sandy Lerner. The router is a device that enables otherwise incompatible computer networks to talk to one another by breaking up data into digestible packets, which it then sends down the correct pipe to its destination. That first router enabled Stanford's computers to communicate with each other. Today, it is estimated that Cisco produces four out of every five routers.

Bosack and Lerner left the company after its initial public stock offering in 1990, turning it over to chairman of the board John Morgridge and chief executive officer John Chambers. Chambers, a man with a finely tuned sense of the sometimes wild arc of high-tech success and failure, was formerly a sales executive at IBM and at Wang Laboratories, Inc. Morgridge, Chambers, and chief information officer Peter Solvik form the visionary team that has built Cisco into the powerhouse it is today—a networking giant that stands shoulder to shoulder with Microsoft and Intel in a triumvirate often playfully referred to "Wintelco."

Think of the Cisco vision in two ways: First, it's the core offering—the products, resources, and expertise; second, it's helping customers remake their companies into fully integrated, network-driven organizations. Cisco calls this comprehensive approach Internetworking and firmly believes it's the wave of the future. Implicit in this vision is a revolutionary level of customization—no two companies will Internetwork in the same way.

Cisco has methodically built itself into a company able to provide such end-to-end integration. This has meant aggressively acquiring companies that manufacture sophisticated hardware. The integration of each new product into Cisco's arsenal meant just that much more capability it could offer customers. In addition, it reduced both their costs and Cisco's.

The next step was to incorporate software. Cisco calls its system the Internetwork Operating System (IOS). The company issues IOS licenses to makers of competing software, similar to the way Microsoft licenses its Windows technology.

The company practices what it preaches. To see how Internetworking works, all a customer need do is look at Cisco itself. Today, Cisco's interfaces with its suppliers are—as *PC Week* described them in a 1997 article—like "permeable membranes" through which suppliers can tap directly into Cisco's systems. This is more a supply *web* than a chain, a set of inter-enterprise processes that seamlessly integrate back-end production, materials management, and distribution.

The Web extends from Cisco's own internal systems to its commercial interaction with customers. Here, Cisco is on the cutting edge of online configuration and customization. With a few mouse clicks, a customer can customize a product or suite of products to meet highly specific, specialized needs. Product support, credit checking, and a host of other services are also available.

It's an online "build-to-order" process. The result is a highly networked enterprise that lowers overhead, gets products to market faster, reduces the cost of goods, and makes for satisfied customers. No wonder Cisco has experienced such explosive growth.

Whether it's supplying the online retail system at Virtual Vineyards, an Internet winery and catalog store; providing a full-service ordering, tracking, and customer service system to US West's !NTERPRISE networking division; or setting up a Virtual Enterprise Program to give students in New York City public schools task-oriented instruction in simulated business environments—Cisco is making Internetwork the gold standard of the Web Rush.

"We do it with fewer people, higher satisfaction, higher differentiation, and higher profitability," says Solvik. "The fundamental reason we're able to do all these things is that we have built an electronic capability to deliver 70 percent of our technical service and support."

Cisco set up its e-commerce program in August 1996, when its employees began using the Internet to improve sales. In the first five months, online selling generated $75 million. By the middle of 1998, that figure topped $15 million a *day.* As this book goes to press, the networking giant projects that fully half of its fiscal year 1998 sales will be online, with Internet revenues of $5 billion.

Impressive as those figures are, that's just the beginning. CEO Chambers predicts that e-commerce will be a trillion-dollar market by the year 2000. In fact, Chambers foresees a day in the not too distant future when successful companies will be almost entirely virtual, and today's Internet will be just one application that runs over a public Internet Protocol (IP) network, much like today's public telephone system. With data, voice, video, and who-knows-what-else residing on the IP network, companies will exist more in Cyberspace than in office space, with radical improvements in productivity, not to mention more immediate, around-the-clock connections to customers.

And online business need not be costly. Cisco has invested a relatively modest $50 million in capital expenditures and spends less than $10 million annually in operating costs—minute figures relative to the company's revenue and market capitalization.

Solvik insists it's a mistake to suppose that most customers aren't ready to get involved with online commerce. "The customer base we're dealing with is technical, and believes in the power of networking," says Solvik. "Fundamentally, we're selling to people who believe that networking on the Internet is going to revolutionize business."

The benefits of such innovation are substantial. Solvik estimates that Cisco itself is eliminating $564 million a year from its operating budget by going online. While no one can promise that other companies will realize equal savings, the evidence is strong that bits and bytes yield greater productivity than phones and faxes. And those savings can be pumped directly into research and development or shared with stakeholders.

Timing is everything, says Solvik. He advises any company thinking about e-commerce to move quickly. Information specialists must transform themselves into network experts, seeking the greatest efficiency from applications. The smoother and more compressed the Internetworking capability, the more flexible the company will become. The key, says Solvik, is to select the Internet technologies that provide the biggest payback at the right moment. The trick, of course, is knowing when that moment is right. Cisco Systems is dedicated to helping companies customize their Internet commerce to the extent that they'll be able to seize that moment—and ride it to new heights of profitability.

❏ *How Cisco clicks with customization:*

1. By building fully integrated, highly sophisticated *inter*networks customized to an organization's specific needs.
2. By prioritizing business opportunities based on customer need.
3. By making highly complex systems understandable and available to companies of all shapes and sizes.

How You Can Click with Customization

- By building Web pages that enable customers to design products and services to fit their needs. Customers who personalize what they buy, as Dell customers do, are likely to feel they have a real investment in and relationship with your company.
- By staying in touch with customer trends. By selling directly over the Internet and eliminating middlemen, a company such as Dell can learn quickly what product or service its customers are looking for next—then take steps to provide it.
- By establishing one-to-one relationships with customers. Make good use of the information your company already has in its database. Track your customers' preferences and buying patterns, then e-mail each customer updates about add-ons or custom features as they become available.
- By speaking the same language as your customers. Dell Online is a good example of a company that tackled the tough job of making its information systems easy to use—it purged company-speak and replaced it with language and applications that civilians can understand.
- By integrating. Nothing exposes malfunctioning processes quicker

than the Internet. If all your business processes aren't in sync, no amount of customization is going to satisfy your customer. Put the company in order before you put it online. Cisco, for instance customized its internal processes prior to going online, and it strongly encourages its customers, shareholders, and resellers to do the same. In other words, customize your company so it fits the Internet.

- By making customization a one-stop shopping experience. Cisco Systems manages to reduce overhead, improve time-to-market, lower the cost, and keep customers satisfied—all because its Internet site encourages one-stop shopping. Link your Web sites and functions so that the customer can travel a well-lit path from one to the next with a click of the mouse, customizing as he or she goes.

- By ensuring accuracy and compatibility in product design. Dell's online customers usually know what they want, but they still make mistakes. You can profit from a support network of troubleshooters who alert customers that the products they have custom designed are dangerous, unworkable, or inefficient.

- By providing timely, purposeful, *customized* communication with your online customers. For the most part, Internet shoppers appreciate e-mails, especially ones that reflect their specific tastes and purchases. They also like updates and information on how to make the products or services they have purchased work better.

6

Click with Savings

Share your savings.
Build your sales.

The growth of the automated teller machine has cut down on trips to the bank for millions of people. But one institution went a step further.

TeleBank, Inc., in Arlington, Virginia, doesn't even have ATMs. Its single branch is home to a pinball machine, not a vault.

Such an unconventional setup would spell disaster for a traditional bank or savings and loan. But, by the third quarter of 1998, TeleBank boasted $2 billion—yes, billion—in assets and 50,000 depositors.

The secret? TeleBank conducts *all* its business via Internet, telephone, fax, mail, or wire. Some 40 percent of all people who contacted TeleBank by late 1998 were doing so online, and the figure was rapidly growing. As a result, the company doesn't have to build branches, ATMs, or maintain any other type of physical structure besides its lone (modest) office. By one analyst's estimate, Telebank's overhead is roughly 1 percent of its assets—considerably less than the 2 or 3 percent average reported for institutions of the same size.

Telebank's plain-vanilla strategy reportedly makes it the lowest-cost producer of banking services in the United States. It also allows the company to pass cost savings along to its customers. This is the savings advantage in action.

Internet customers reap the benefit of Internet companies reducing their own costs of production and distribution. Sites all over the Web offer cheap prices on everything from airfares to automobiles, from bath towels to umbrellas. For bargain-hunters, the Internet is fast becoming the biggest candy store in this galaxy.

Who has the savings advantage?

Northwest Airlines Company uses the Internet to cut its ticketing costs by more than 80 percent. Then it passes along a chunk of its savings to its Web customers, offering them significant discounts on fares.

BMG Direct, Inc., a division of BMG Entertainment, sells CDs and tapes to online customers at substantial savings over what they would pay in a retail store. How BMG's Web site became the little engine that could makes an interesting study in business psychology.

At first, senior managers considered the site a minor indulgence. Then the revenue results started coming in. Talk about profits! And wasn't everybody at BMG always in favor of Internet business? Of course they were.

And you will be, too.

Northwest Airlines Clicks with Savings

Every Wednesday at 12:01 A.M., the rush begins. Thousands of people bolt to their PCs, power them up, and log onto the Internet in search of spurof-the-moment vacations. To what Web site are these hungry pilgrims flocking? Northwest Airline's www.na.com, where the world's fourth-largest carrier lists its weekly CyberSaver tickets at fares of up to 85 percent off.

Judging from the weekly numbers—several hundred thousand come to check and over two thousand buy—many of these night-owl consumers are going away satisfied. Although CyberSavers are restricted to flights leaving the following Saturday and returning Monday or Tuesday, the prices are so low that within forty-eight hours most seats are sold. The planes cost Northwest the same amount to fly no matter how many people are on board, so the company benefits from every empty seat filled, as long as no full-fare passengers are turned away. In fact, this quick infusion of customers is a tremendous revenue generator even with tickets selling at rock-bottom rates.

Since launching its Web site in April 1996, the Eagan, Minnesota–based company has accomplished a number of online objectives. The first airline carrier to allow frequent flyers to book travel over the Internet, Northwest gives all its customers that option today. But the airline has hardly forgotten its frequent flyers—they now have their own private e-forum. Most important, the company offers great value with its Internet-only discounts and CyberSavers listings, circumventing travel agents (and their fees) and building customer loyalty and excitement.

When the federal government deregulated prices on commercial airline travel in 1978, it set the stage for fare wars. Skirmishes continue to this day, much to the delight of passengers. The computerized reservation system known as SABRE, developed in 1964 by American Airlines, enabled travel agents to track rates across the industry. As a result, from 1978 to 1988, the percentage of tickets bought through agents—as opposed to directly from the airlines—rose from 30 percent to 80 percent, according to Al Lenza, vice president of distribution planning at Northwest Airlines. The alternative was calling the airlines on an almost daily basis to check for deals, a task for which few travelers had either the time or patience. Under the new system, finding the best deal possible was the objective, but it was the agents—who typically earned sizable commissions for every ticket they sold—who were happiest.

The Internet, however, quickly rewrote this scenario. Now, instead of leaving their fate in the hands of agents, an increasing number of industrious travelers hunt for their own bargains using essentially the same technology. And since airlines can now market directly to the end user, designing a Web site that updates fare information is a sensible thing to do.

When Al Lenza joined Northwest in 1994, a small group within information services at the airline was already at work designing a mostly informational Web site, but other divisions, including marketing, showed little interest in the project. Lenza built support throughout the organization—after twelve years working on Continental Airlines' computer reservations system, he knew a lot about how to leverage technology.

Designing a site is a company-wide initiative that requires everyone's involvement, says Lenza. "In the initial going at Northwest, it was convenient for everybody to just say, 'Oh, that's the Internet guy's problem,' or 'Let Al take care of it.' Although I own the overall success or failure of this project, a company's Web site shouldn't be owned by electronic commerce or distribution alone. It needs a cross-functional team intent on making sure every piece of value the company has to offer—be that its reservation system, frequent flyer programs, or its customer service—is well represented."

Lenza and his team established three core objectives for the site. First, the company wanted to establish a stronger bond with its preferred customers—frequent flyers. Second, it wanted to sell everything that it normally sold over the phone and in person—at a lower cost. And third, it wanted to reduce distribution costs. This would be accomplished as more customers ordered tickets electronically, saving the airline paper and processing costs. "E-ticketed" customers would go straight to the gate and simply show a photo ID to secure their seats, or use a self-service kiosk.

When Northwest began researching its foray onto the Web in 1995, less than 1 percent of all airline bookings were made online. Undeterred, Northwest's cross-functional team of Information Services, Marketing, and Distributor Planning focused on its core objectives while simultaneously launching an informational resource site in April 1996.

Though the initial site lacked booking and purchasing capabilities, it did offer schedules, flight information, e-mail access to consumer relations, and a frequent flyer center where customers could check their WorldPerks mileage points. There were also weather reports issued by the Weather Channel, and updates on CyberSavers that could then be purchased by calling a toll-free number.

"The site was interactive to some degree, but it wasn't yet a fully functional distribution channel—which was our overriding objective," says Lenza. "You still had to pick up the phone to actually acquire any of the things that we were telling you about." Even with this limitation, however, Northwest's site generated plenty of activity: During its first month of operation it received 1.6 million hits.

In early 1997 Northwest established a partnership with Microsoft Travel Technologies. The software included, as Lenza explains, "front-end pieces that walked a customer through the booking process." Today, visitors to the site can not only book reservations on all Northwest's domestic and international flights, they can also peruse multimedia travel guides and even reserve hotel rooms and rental cars. These services have proven so successful that other major airlines—including American, Continental, and TWA—are now offering similar services on their Web sites.

The first month its online reservations system was in operation, Northwest averaged 35 to 40 tickets sold per day. A year later, during the first quarter of 1998, over 700 tickets were sold daily and the number now approaches 1,000. Lenza predicts the company could generate $100 million in online revenue by year's end—not bad for a return on an investment of less than $5 million.

Like all airlines, Northwest is dependent on the revenue base provided by its frequent flyers—who still account for approximately two-thirds of all visitors to the site. In 1998, Northwest initiated a system designed to strengthen its relationships with these jet jockeys by e-mailing them personalized offerings, including savings at hotels and restaurants in cities they visit often. When a major sale is imminent, frequent flyers will know about it a day early and get first pick. Frequent flyers will get advance notice of new routes so they can prepare for the additional flight options. And there will be a customized notification system—if Lois Marsh of Boston has family in Los Angeles, for instance, she'll be notified whenever cheap flights to Southern California pop up. Combining convenience and customization with great savings, Northwest looks to keep its customer base secure and loyal.

As discussed earlier, there are considerable cost savings on every ticket sold over the Internet. Northwest pays an average of $32 for every ticket sold through an agent. When it happens online, the cost is a mere six dollars. In March 1998, Northwest began passing these savings on to its Internet customers in the form of an additional $20 discount per ticket.

The result was dramatic. Before the discount, 70 percent of users still chose to log off and dial Northwest's toll-free number to buy their tickets. Within a few weeks, 80 percent were booking their trips online.

This is evidence not only of the universal love of a bargain, but also of the typical Internet user's desire for control. "Price is a big motivator, as well as control," agrees Lenza. "We've found in our research that an overwhelming percentage of people just don't feel they're getting the best deal, whether it's through their travel agent or the telephone. They want to see for themselves. They want to shop. They want control. And they're willing to pay for it in terms of spending their own time."

A particular priority for Northwest at the moment is attracting business travelers from small companies. These customers will be offered discounts, upgrades, or some combination of benefits to encourage increased online patronage, as well as given spreadsheets that record and report their monthly travel.

Overall, the Northwest site is the linchpin of what the company anticipates will be a general shift to customer self-service. Travelers at nineteen airports can now obtain their own boarding pass or change their seat or flight at self-serve kiosks. The process cuts down on waiting time, and frees up Northwest gate personnel to deal with more pressing customer concerns. As of mid-1998, more than 100,000 customers are using the machines each week.

"For us, distribution costs go beyond the saving of a commission or the facilitating of a self-serve booking transaction," says Lenza. "It goes to reducing paper ticket expenses, reducing the wait time for customers to do business with Northwest, and reducing lines at the airports so people can go right through. Ideally, all Northwest travelers will have to do is check their bags."

Like many companies, Northwest is discovering that its Internet presence can create collateral opportunities to reduce costs and pass savings along to customers. Customers reap substantial savings, and the company profits from their gain.

❏ *How Northwest Airlines clicks with savings:*

1. By filling up undersold flights online through its excitement-creating CyberSavers.
2. By leveraging its Internet presence to further automate its processes—thereby cutting costs and passing the savings on to customers.
3. By reducing its dependence on travel agents.

BMG Entertainment Clicks with Savings

As the Internet began its explosive growth in the mid-1990s, executives at BMG Direct (www.bmgmusicservice.com), formerly RCA Direct Marketing Inc. dba RCA Music Service, knew they faced both a threat and an opportunity. For decades their company had sold its records, tapes, and CDs mostly by mail order, and the Web looked like a logical extension of that marketplace. But BMG Direct wasn't sure of the best way to approach the billion-dollar behemoth.

"So many of the companies getting attention for e-commerce are Internet-centric," says Elizabeth Rose, vice president of strategic planning and electronic commerce. "But the real challenge—and frankly where the hype and disappointment are greatest—is when companies with existing businesses struggle to adapt to the medium."

BMG Direct is a classic example of a company that has found its Web way through trial and error. Underfunded and underdeveloped, its first site was largely dysfunctional. But then the company demonstrated its commitment by replacing its leadership—and things have turned around. As of mid-1998 it had 500,000 online members and was adding about 100,000 new ones each month. The Internet currently accounts for around 2 percent of annual revenue, a number that is expected to rise dramatically as the company speeds up its mailing services and its customers grow comfortable with the Web.

A division of BMG Entertainment—a $6 billion company with music, film, TV, and media storage interests—BMG Direct has a decades-long history of success in direct mail, an industry that has always been (and for the most part still is) dependent on paper. With over eight million members, BMG's sole rival in the music industry is Columbia House.

The traditional value proposition of music clubs is a simple one. A consumer gets several free CDs or tapes for joining, and accepts some level of commitment to make additional purchases at club rates. Then a catalog comes about every three weeks with a featured selection based on the consumer's music preferences. Within a certain number of days, the member has to say "yes" or "no"; if there's no response, the selection is sent automatically. This so-called "negative option" conditions members to open their club mail—and open it quickly. Customers often then order other products from the catalog.

The negative option has worked as a marketing paradigm for half a century, driving book clubs as well as music clubs. Members actively engage and bond with their clubs, and the clubs learn their tastes and cater to them. Costs and procedures, percentages of acceptance, refusal, and random purchase, all have long since been analyzed and tested into certainty. By its successful use of this model, BMG Direct has become the number one music club in the United States.

In April 1996, in what Rose calls a "classic example of 'Hey Gang, let's put up a Web site,'" BMG Direct went online in an offhand manner. A couple of junior people within the company—given a mandate not to spend much money or distract from the "real business"—put up a simple site that allowed members to search the product list and respond to featured selections. But while it provided an outpost for computer-active members and brought in 2,600 new members per month, the site had a number of problems.

During the time traditionally allowed for response to a mailing, members can accumulate two or even three more mailings, each with its own featured selection. The BMG Direct Web site was only able to recognize one mailing at a time. This confused members and resulted in myriad mixups where the wrong selection was sent. In addition, customers had to have their account number with them each time they went online, and American Online subscribers couldn't use the site at all unless they had installed Netscape Navigator.

"It was a klutzy site to use," Rose says frankly, "and we got flame mail from members about how horrible it was." A small percentage of these electronic diatribes also made it clear that Columbia House had a better site. Here the competitive aspects of the Internet became painfully palpable—members were being lost.

On the other hand, as bad as the site was, people were still visiting—members were struggling through the difficulties to make as many as thirty thousand transactions a month. The senior people at the company paid attention; they knew they were onto something, and they knew it needed to be taken seriously.

Rose came to the company at the end of 1996 and assumed responsibility for the site. Her priorities included basic usability and accessibility, as well as a remedy for the mailing cycle confusion. But before plunging in, Rose stepped back and spent a couple of months pondering long-term strategies.

With the traditional paper-based process, members mail in their selection card—and then have no mechanism for ordering until the next catalog comes. If they hear a song they love and *have* to have the disc, they rush out to Tower Records and BMG has lost a sale. With the Internet, the company could establish an ongoing dialog. Customers could order anytime—the feature selection would be just one part of the relationship. They could take advantage of sale offers and review the entire catalog of twelve thousand titles rather than the six hundred in the typical print catalog.

An entirely new BMG Direct site went up in January 1998. It was designed for clarity, ease, and fun—and along with the features described above, offers snippets from the latest songs and discs and conveniences like address and preference changes. Using instant sales feedback, the site flags best sellers for members. It also informs them of sales and special promotions, and prints reviews and commentary.

Once BMG Direct feels absolutely sure that it can sell, and keep selling, to people exclusively online, Rose plans to offer members a no-paper, all-electronic option. For the time being, though, she is pleased at having won the company 100,000 new members as of June 1998—a goal reached largely through Web word of mouth.

Many of these members are Internet aficionados and would probably have ended up at Columbia House if BMG hadn't gotten its act together. An added plus—online users place orders that are on average 35 percent larger.

Is the site perfect? No. For one thing, it's incapable of tracking a customer's course through the site—a process Rose calls "path analysis." Effective path analysis would deliver a wealth of data about site use and customer interest, and Rose puts it at the top of her wish list.

Rose also voices irritation at the notion that the Internet, almost of its own volition, will divine a customer's needs and deliver personalized attention. Rose has no doubt that the Internet can respond to customers dynamically and with a high degree of customization, but she has also learned that "each and every dynamic reaction of the site has to have programming behind it." The development and implementation of this programming accounts for the price difference between the original site and the new one—$200,000 versus $2 million. Monthly maintenance costs are $15,000 to $20,000.

Rose understands that it takes a serious investment of resources, money, and commitment to move companies with long paper-trail histories onto the Internet. And BMG has a way to go. Billing and distribution are all still oriented to paper. Integrating these online may lag until e-commerce has grown enough to justify the expense. And perhaps ten years out the historic challenge will emerge: Managing sales of a product, music, that can be downloaded directly into members' computers.

Meanwhile, BMG Direct has staked a claim on the Internet and is ready to welcome a swelling migration. It has retained customers it might have lost to Internet competition, and this is crucial in the music business where growth has been nearly static. In short, BMG is an example of a traditional company making the often difficult but always necessary move to the Web.

❏ *How BMG Entertainment clicks with savings:*

1. By attracting customers that would have been lost to its competitors.
2. By building a continuous electronic dialog with customers that enables them to order at any time, as opposed to only during the company's traditional catalog cycles.
3. By reducing paper and mailing costs.

How You Can Click with Savings

- By selling your surplus products at bargain rates. Use the Internet to advertise time-sensitive products, as Northwest Airlines does. That way, you avoid absorbing the full costs of unsold goods or services.
- By underselling your competitors who only sell in stores. Selling to customers on its Web site, a company such as BMG Direct can cut operating costs and deliver its product less expensively than its competitors—and still make a profit.
- By integrating traditional business functions into your Web site technology that save time and money. This way, you speed up your processes and avoid duplication. As BMG testifies, each feature of the Web site requires programming designed from a business perspective.
- By spending money to save money. This old adage may be a cliché, but it is also a reality. A Web site that saves customers money, BMG shows, will raise some of your costs. The art is to integrate as many of your business processes as possible into your Web technology, so that you can realize compensatory savings.

7

Click with Community

Connect your customers.
Create a community.

Utopia is "no place"—literally. Thomas More coined the word in 1516 (using the Greek *ou* for no and *topos* for place) to describe an ideal community where everyone's interests are aligned. More was being ironic. He meant that no such place could exist anywhere on earth.

More is probably still right about earth itself. But not to put too fine a line on it, Internet enthusiasts might now argue that Utopian communities actually do exist—in cyberspace. Online communities arise and thrive out there in the ether every day. All it takes is a small crowd of computer users discovering a mutual interest they are willing to share, discuss, and change when necessary.

Establishing and nurturing such communities can be a rich source of advantage, provided participants are treated with respect. If some people's mutual interests strike you as off the wall, keep it to yourself. Be glad they comprise a market you can reach.

In this chapter, we examine four businesses that have captured the community advantage. GeoCities has established dozens of different neighborhoods on its Web site. These areas appeal to people of all ages and backgrounds, who share specific interests—from business to baseball, pets to politics.

SeniorNet, a nonprofit organization, captures the community advantage by defying conventional wisdom that older people resist technology. The organization gives older people who are not yet computer literate the opportunity to learn personal-computer skills from their peers.

Purple Moon has captured the community advantage by appealing to girls ages eight to twelve and giving them an arena to share their thoughts and feelings. The site offers a number of activities and products designed with just them in mind.

Women.com captures the community advantage by providing a forum for women to talk about money, investing, health, news, beauty, fashion, shopping, and careers.

GeoCities Clicks with Community

The city never sleeps—and neither does GeoCities, Inc. (www.geocities.com). According to recent Media Matrix rankings, one out of every four people who go online visits its pacesetting Web site. Its population stood at nearly two million as of mid-1998, and more than ten thousand new subscribers are added each day. Every month fourteen million visitors scroll its streets, checking out what's happening in the neighborhoods. Yes, the lure of urban living is strong—even if the city is virtual.

Founded in 1995, GeoCities bills itself as the "largest and fastest-growing community on the Internet." Many of its basic services—e-mail, chat groups, file management, and technical support—are free, and each user is provided 11 megabytes of space to create his or her own Web page. Members who wish more storage space—up to 25 megabytes, plus their own URL (universe resource locator) address—pay a monthly membership fee of $4.95. The site also offers entrepreneurs a place to do business—small businesses can take advantage of GeoCities' commerce solutions for about $25 a month. These include Web-page creation, credit card transactions, and links to other sites. All in all, GeoCities provides a vast community where people can meet, share ideas, argue, laugh, shop, and even fall in love.

GeoCities' vice president and general manager Richard Rygg discusses the site's popularity and phenomenal growth: "The Web came along and turbocharged people's ability to express themselves. One of the most basic facts of human nature is that people find other people interesting and want to interact with them, and GeoCities allows them to communicate in a number of different ways."

The site capitalizes on a basic human need to connect—a need that television, radio, and film have never been able to fulfill. "Talk radio" comes close, and some television shows invite callers to respond to discussions or cast "votes" by telephone, but neither can offer the immediate gratification and freewheeling interaction of the Web.

Although users enjoy a measure of anonymity, GeoCities stresses general Internet etiquette: no bigotry, nudity, illegal activities, or defamation. Visitors are asked to support GeoCities' advertisers and to acknowledge GeoCities as the host on member-created Web pages.

As its name implies, GeoCities is organized around the concept of a city—not a city of bridges and towers, but a virtual, global city. London was the great city of the nineteenth century and New York of the twenti-eth—will CyberCity earn that mantle in the twenty-first century? People who "move" to GeoCities are referred to as "homesteaders." They join the throng along fourteen "avenues"—among them Arts and Literature, Automobiles, Business, Family, Sports, and Travel. Each avenue leads to a group of "neighborhoods," some forty in all, where people with common interests connect. One neighborhood is "Athens," bubbling with educa-tion, literature, poetry, and philosophy; another is "TelevisionCity," where fans gather to rave and rant about Calista, Clooney, Cokie, and Sam. Somewhat further afield are the "suburbs," where visitors pay visits to the home pages of individuals and small businesses.

The city metaphor is applied throughout the GeoCities site—and public transportation has never been as painless. Each neighborhood has a core group of volunteer community leaders ready to help newcomers build a home page or find technical support, or just to provide moral en-couragement to the Net novice. This sense of community is an enormous attraction. Because the neighborhoods are self-defined and self-created, there is a sense of democracy and egalitarianism about the site: It's built by the people for the people. As Rygg notes, "By letting our members build their own community, we are strengthening their sense of owner-ship. The less we do, the better. They build it—they own it."

This hands-off policy doesn't mean that GeoCities managers aren't on top of things. Each month, executives from the head office—including founder David Bohnett, CEO Tom Evans, and Rich Rygg—conduct a con-ference call with community leaders from all over the world. They want to know what's working and what isn't, what people love and what they hate. But when someone unsavory slinks into a neighborhood, community leaders don't wait for the monthly meeting. The interlopers are quickly given the boot. It's important to retain a sense of order and civility in the Wild Wild Web.

And GeoCities is winning on the Web. The company divides its revenue streams into three basic categories: advertising, commissions, and premium services. Homesteaders agree to allow banner advertising on their home pages; neighborhoods have a say in what billboards go up on their block. Companies who sell on the site—including Amazon.com, Surplus Direct (formerly Egghead), CDnow, and First USA—pay a commission. Value-added services—helping small businesses set up shop and processing their transactions—is the third revenue stream.

By mid-1998, advertising generated approximately 80 percent of revenue. However, the company foresees that changing as partnerships and premium services grow. As Bohnett explains, "We've already got a pretty good toehold in both those other areas, and it's just a matter of time before they even out the revenue percentages."

With revenue increasing by more than 400 percent in 1998, it's obvious that GeoCities is a happening place. As Rygg says, "This is just the beginning. The Internet is creating not global villages, but global metropolises. The potential for growth is astounding." An historic "virtual" migration has begun—and, like all great movements of people, it is ripe with commercial opportunity.

❏ *How GeoCities clicks with community:*

1. By providing newcomers with guides who welcome them into the community and help them build their own online presence.

2. By enabling and encouraging a global dialog on issues large and small.

3. By building virtual Main Streets where members can stroll, browse, and shop.

SeniorNet Clicks with Community

America is graying—there is no segment of the population growing at a faster rate than senior citizens. By the year 2010, 115 million of us will be drawing Social Security checks and, if SeniorNet (www.seniornet.org) has anything to say about it, doing most of our shopping on the Internet.

Defying pundits who say that seniors are technophobic, many older citizens have already joined virtual communities. "We very quickly punctured the myth that seniors fear computers," says SeniorNet president Ann Wrixon. "It is true that seniors don't have much fun trying to learn from instructors in their twenties, who presume a lifelong familiarity with computers rather than anticipating, say, the potential difficulty someone with arthritis may have manipulating a mouse."

Based in San Francisco, SeniorNet has worked for more than a decade to create an e-community for older adults. It all began in 1986 as a student project at the University of San Francisco, led by Professor Mary Furlong. Furlong remembered how much her grandmother had enjoyed visiting a park near her home, where she sat on a bench with her friends and chatted and gossiped. The professor and her students set out to see if technology could generate and support a "park bench" community.

The project began with a dial-up system called the Delphi Network that connected seniors at five different sites. One of the first challenges was to teach them how to use something that was entirely foreign to them. Furlong bought inexpensive computers, set up workshops in church basements, senior centers, nursing homes, and local schools, and quickly had all the pupils she could handle. The students quickly mastered the requisite technology and proved eager to share the intangible wealth of their life experiences.

By small increments, the SeniorNet community began to grow. Helped by public and corporate funding, it established a network of more than 140 learning centers in schools, malls, hospitals, community centers, housing projects, and senior centers throughout the United States. SeniorNet became one of the original content providers to America Online, and by 1991 its membership had grown to 20,000.

In 1995, SeniorNet formally established itself as a nonprofit organization for adults aged fifty and older who wanted to learn new computer skills and discuss topics related to aging. Today membership approaches 28,000, with an annual fee of $35. The site offers computer courses, costing an average of $35, the revenue from which goes to support local centers.

SeniorNet Web members—as well as casual visitors—can take online classes; find bargains on computers, health newsletters, and books; read columns; meet folks who share their hobbies and passions; and find out about site-sponsored cruises to Alaska and the Caribbean. By far the most popular areas, however, are the SeniorNet RoundTables—fifty interest-based arenas holding more than 350 discussion groups on every imaginable topic. Health naturally attracts a good deal of attention, but books and literature attract even more. Wrixon also notes that "serious groups dealing with dying, death, and bereavement attract extraordinary numbers of committed participants."

With baby boomers aging by the millions, SeniorNet's future looks rosy indeed. One in three adults aged fifty-five or older now owns a computer. A recent CommerceNet/Nielsen study found that there are thirteen million Internet users over the age of fifty in the United States and Canada—a nearly 50 percent jump in less than two years. Over 42 percent of computer users aged sixty-five and older have bought items over the Internet—the highest percentage of any age group. And as SeniorNet evolves, it is developing online advertising.

Despite its successes, SeniorNet members renew at a rate of only 35 percent. Although this may at first seem to indicate problems, it should be remembered that SeniorNet's stated objective is to educate people so that they can travel the highways of the Internet on their own. Many of the 100,000 seniors who have profited from SeniorNet's instruction discover that they no longer need the benefits of membership.

SeniorNet currently relies on three annual revenue streams: $500,000 from membership fees, $500,000 from funds raised for new local sites around the country, and $500,000 from corporate and foundation grants. For the next five years the organization will focus on opening new Learning Centers and establishing a self-sustaining momentum.

As the foremost senior organization on the Internet, SeniorNet has earned plenty of recognition, offering its members important services they are hard-pressed to find elsewhere. Corporate sponsors like IBM, MetLife, Charles Schwab, Ameritech, and Microsoft have been loyal and generous. To its sponsors, the site presents a distinct commercial value by allowing them to target a large and growing market. Most important, the site has made a difference in the lives of many. Imagine you're seventy-five years old, wheelchair bound, living in isolation. Suddenly, that park bench and all the warmth and community it holds is just a click away.

❏ *How SeniorNet clicks with community:*

1. By providing a virtual park bench where seniors can meet and mingle.
2. By setting up learning centers that teach computer skills and enlarge the e-community.
3. By bringing together seniors in a nonthreatening environment where they discuss issues ranging from recipes to mortality.

Purple Moon Clicks with Community

Purple Moon (www.purple-moon.com) is a site built expressly for girls ages eight to twelve. It grew out of the debate over what psychological and intellectual qualities distinguish males from females, as well as what contribution culture makes to the development of these differences. Books such as Carol Gilligan's *In a Different Voice* (Harvard University Press, 1993) have drawn attention to the cultural factors that encourage males to be more logic-oriented, while females place greater value on re-lationships.

In 1992, Interval Research Corporation spotted a gender gap in the evolving profile of computer users. Research, news reports, and anecdo-tal evidence suggested that boys used computers widely from a young age, both for learning and for fun, and were then translating their skills into jobs and enhanced work performance. Girls were lagging behind.

The people who founded Purple Moon recognized this discrepancy and set out to remedy it. Brenda Laurel, then a research fellow at Interval with a distinguished twenty-year career in entertainment software and research, embarked on a major study of gender differences, play patterns, and technology usage among girls and boys aged eight to twelve. Laurel and her research team reviewed the relevant literature, then spent thousands of hours interviewing boys and girls, as well as teachers, scout leaders, arcade managers, computer game retailers, and the country's leading experts in play and gender difference. They identified a community woefully underserved by the Internet—namely, young girls—and created a site designed to fill this gap in an educational manner.

Laurel and her team discovered that girls do appreciate computers and computer games, but differently from boys. In general, girls find violence-driven games boring and simplistic, preferring games that involve role playing, creativity, skill building, and problem solving. Before Purple Moon, however, there was nothing on the Internet that came close to appealing to these interests.

In adventure games, the team discovered girls are captivated not by super-heroes but by everyday people—as real to girls as their best friends. The goal is not to win, but to explore, to have new experiences with varying outcomes. Speed and action aren't the key; sensory immersion and strong story lines are. Girls prefer complex narratives and real-life settings. And success comes not through the elimination of competitors, but through the development of relationships. Girls are profoundly social, an attribute that—through multiplayer games, e-mail, and chat rooms—can easily be addressed by the Internet.

In September 1996, Interval Research announced the formation of Purple Moon. The site is self-contained and rigorously monitored for safety. Girls spend time with the Purple Moon characters, find out about Whistling Pines Junior High, and interact with other members. They can set up personal Web sites; send virtual postcards; collect virtual treasures such as flowers or exotic stones and then send them to other girls; and shop for actual exotic stones, CD-ROMs, character dolls, and Purple Moon products.

Purple Moon relies principally on three sources of revenue: CD-ROM sales in off-site stores, Internet sponsorships, and online sales. The largest percentage comes from the off-site CD-ROM sales. Sales of girls' CD-ROMs in general grew a phenomenal 250 percent in 1997, and Nancy Deyo, Purple Moon president and CEO, projects that "the total sales figure will reach $135 million in 1998, with Purple Moon capturing nearly 10 percent of that market." During the 1997 holiday season, Purple Moon's CD-ROMs were among the top fifty selling titles, competing against such blockbusters as Riven, Microsoft Flight Simulator, and Tomb Raider. The only other girls' titles to appear on the list were American Girl and Barbie, which have twelve and forty years respectively of brand equity.

Purple Moon gave a good deal of thought to the delicate issue of advertising in a community of children. The company chose to offer sponsorships outside the narrative adventure games, in areas such as the Treasure Trove. Bonne Bell has been the prototype sponsor, offering "themed" treasures like its popular Smackers lip gloss. Other sponsors include SeaWorld, the chain of aquatic parks, which offers limited-edition, sea-themed treasures in connection with the Secret Path to the Sea CD-ROM. Day Runner, the industry leader in paper-based organizers and organizing tools, offers Purple Moon planners, pens, and character stickers; Fossil watches does the same with its product. At current monthly rates of $15,000 for 450,000 hits and $10,500 for 350,000,

Purple Moon guarantees the number of times that an advertisement will be seen.

Purple Moon has learned that girls—and their parents—are attracted to one-site online shopping. "The idea," according to Nancy Deyo, "is to develop a pervasive fan culture around Purple Moon and its characters. It's already the premiere Web site for girls, and aims to become a primary destination for every girl every day." During Purple Moon's first year, site orders had to be phoned in. In the fall of 1998, however, it started direct online sales. Parents appreciate the site's use of permission agreements, gift certificates, and wish lists.

In just under two years, the Purple Moon site recorded 106 million hits; it has 150,000 registered users and is adding 10,000 to 15,000 more every month. Users typically visit the site three times every two days for between thirty and forty minutes each time, touching an average of fifty pages. More than 3.7 million virtual treasures have been exchanged, and 7 million virtual postcards have been sent.

The market responded quickly to Purple Moon, thanks to diligent research and the ingenuity of its founders—who recognized a community that was not well served on the Internet and set about to correct the omission. It approached this marketplace with maturity and sensitivity, never losing sight of its responsibility to America's young women.

❑ *How Purple Moon clicks with community:*

1. By focusing on an underserved population and developing a Web to meet their needs.
2. By creating a secure and sensitive site where girls can grow and learn.

3. By maintaining rigorous standards on advertising and promotions—never losing sight of its educational mission.

Women.com Networks Clicks with Community

As Internet access exploded in the 1990s, one fact stood out: Most of the users were males. Perhaps this shouldn't be surprising, given that so many Web sites were devoted to computer wares and other traditionally male-oriented fields. Female users received little attention, and when they did venture into cyberspace, many encountered a hostile environment of technical jargon and sexual innuendo.

Seeing both the promise of the Internet and its lack of gender equity, Ellen Pack founded Women's Wire in 1992. Originally a dial-up service, operating over a proprietary communication system, Women's Wire offered subscribers the opportunity to chat and post messages within a closed community. Growth peaked at around fifteen hundred—and then Pack hired Marleen McDaniel, who had considerable Internet experience. The pair brought in a staff of writers and editors, then set out to design a Web site centered on eight subjects: money and investing, health, news, entertainment, beauty, fashion, shopping, and careers.

From the start, Women.com Networks (www.women.com) was intent on creating a community and offering it content that was relevant, stimulating, and practical. The site grew fast: By mid-1998, it had expanded into a network of seven linked sites attracting three million visitors a month. The company was also generating close to $10 million in annual revenue, 90 percent of it from advertisers eager to reach a well-defined demographic: college-educated women with average annual incomes of $60,000. The site is expected to start making a profit sometime in 1999.

"These are smart, well-educated, high-income women, diverse in their interests. They don't want to be stereotyped," explains McDaniel, president and CEO of the San Mateo, California–based company. "In order to build a strong community, we had to give them the resources they wanted. Each of the eight topics was a center of gravity around which to build, and over time, as we've listened to the thousands of e-mails we get each month, we've developed an editorial voice—a position that we believe the Women.com woman represents."

These women are busy, they're engaged, and they're curious—and they want to enrich their lives. The MoneyMode site helps them manage their portfolios and gives investment advice. The Healthy Ideas site (www.healthyideas.com) helps them make sense of the avalanche of information about herbal supplements; the Stork Site (www.storksite.com) makes pregnancy easier. And once baby arrives, the Crayola FamilyPlay site (www.familyplay.com) points them to the best toys. There is even a site that keeps members up-to-date on what's hot elsewhere on the Web—Beatrice's Web Guide (www.bguide.com).

Independent communities have grown up within each of the sites, thanks to more than 170 chat rooms and bulletin boards. Experts on a site's particular subject keep "office hours" during which they answer questions, keep people focused, and start up new discussions. At the Stork Site a registered nurse is on call and volunteer "mentor moms" are on hand to help other women whose due date is approaching.

"Our users are extremely vocal," says McDaniel. "We get thousands of e-mails each month, which help build content and shape the communities. We've learned that pregnant women are very interested in talking with others who have been through the experience, so we've put a lot of emphasis on our mentor moms. It's very important for the users to feel they're in charge of their area."

To engender this feeling of ownership, Women.com embeds interactive tools and actively seeks input. Rather than just showing a selection of the latest coats—à la Vogue—users are asked, "Here are the coats being offered by five designers this fall. Click on the ones you would wear." McDaniel jokes that the current-events questionnaires cover topics ranging from "Barbie to Bosnia," and says they are among the most popular features. Then there are the no-holds-barred town meetings. "We use the interactivity to make people feel more a part of things," McDaniel says, "and it works."

Revenues come from banner ads and sponsorships—such as the Excedrin Headache Research Center—plus promotions and contests that offer the chance to win a car, a vacation, or a shopping spree. Sears ran a special Father's Day promotion for its Craftsman line in 1998 that was among the company's most successful web-based promotions. Why? Because, contrary to popular conception, fully two thirds of all tool buyers are women.

To create an additional revenue stream, Women.com has launched an online store that sells books, vitamins, workout videos, and even furniture. The store generated only about 10 percent of the company's revenue as of mid-1998, but McDaniel expects this figure to increase significantly as it moves from affiliate sales relationships to direct selling through distributors.

The number of visitors to Women.com has continued to grow by 10 to 20 percent each month, but McDaniel says it's getting harder and more expensive to maintain this rate of growth. She says the company is considering adding additional sites for teenagers and young girls. Each site will be designed with the same careful attention to market research that has made the initial seven sites so successful.

"In the last decade, during the feminist movement, what women wanted was empowerment," says McDaniel. "Today we assume we're empowered. So now the focus is on exploring the deeper themes about who we are and how we can leverage our assets. Our users have named us 'The Smart Network.' That's what we want to remain."

Women.com offers companies a preview of how they can shape their message and their e-media to capitalize on the ever-increasing power of women.

❏ *How Women Networks clicks with community:*

1. By listening to its users and giving them a large say in the shape of the site.
2. By creating interactivity in its commercial offerings through preference polls and chat rooms.
3. By supplying topic-specific experts and mentors to build trust and foster real-time dialog.

How You Can Click with Community

- By creating an online community. The Internet allows you to foster closer connections with your customers. It also promotes interaction among your customers. In the process, you build new streams of revenue.
- By encouraging interest-specific online communities. By doing this, you can create a defined market—and not only for your own goods

and services. Sites, such as GeoCities, sell advertisers access to these target audiences.

- By finding pools of potential customers who haven't yet discovered the Internet and bringing them online. As SeniorNet has shown, an organization can generate excitement for the Internet among a new group of users, even those who have no previous computer experience—then target these users with products and services. Purple Moon has shown how a company can create a community online and establish an identity as a key purveyor of products and services to that community.

- By taking advantage of already existing online communities to market your products and services. Provide links between your Web site and the online groups to encourage free and rapid passage from one site to another. Such links are the arteries that will keep life-giving revenues flowing into your business.

- By allowing the members of a community to develop a sense of ownership and control. All successful sites provide some means of responding—bulletin boards, e-mail, chat rooms—but users have to see evidence that their comments and suggestions are being heard. The watchword is interactive.

- By hiring experts to manage interactive communication with your customers. Women.com uses subject-matter experts to keep users focused on the topic at hand and to answer their questions.

- By learning how the needs of community members are changing and finding ways of adapting to them. Life, as well as business, is interesting because people's needs are forever changing. By the same token, communities change, and as a result so must the Web sites that purport to serve them.

8

Click with Entertainment

Make it fun.
Make it pay.

Entertainment pays.

Just ask the people at Berkeley Systems, Inc.

In 1996, the entertainment software giant commissioned a study on the potential impact of advertising over the Internet. In the process, it learned a lot about the people who were buying and playing its games online.

For starters, its customers were older (average age thirty-one) and better-educated (82 percent had attended college) than expected. Also, their professional status and annual incomes averaging $54,000 made them prime prospects for high-end consumer goods.

In sum, these weren't just teenage video game players with modest disposal incomes. Armed with this information, Berkeley Systems had little trouble finding companies willing to advertise on its site.

This chapter profiles businesses that leverage their Web sites by using entertainment to draw customers. These days, Berkeley Systems does it with games such as You Don't Know Jack, in which users can chat with other online contestants while engaged in a rapid-fire quiz show. Marketing itself as "humorous, intelligent entertainment for grown-ups," the company has found a way to help its customers make friends and have fun at the same time.

Brøderbund Software, Inc., also captures the entertainment advantage with games, including the two best-sellers of all-time—Myst and Riven. Once drawn in, Brøderbund visitors are likely to become customers for the company's new products and real-time ordering system.

IBM Corporation captures the entertainment advantage, too. At the height of the 1998 Winter Games, its Nagano Olympics Web site received more than fifty million hits per day from fans looking for event information or results, chatting, and sending messages to athletes. Even though use of the site was free and IBM sold nothing on it directly, the exposure was a terrific public relations move for the company—and a great public service.

CBS SportsLine (SPLN) captures the entertainment advantage by offering Internet users a place to go for sports information, merchandise, and conversation. Jam-packed with everything from news and statistics to audio and video clips, it can also link users to a multitude of sports books, jobs, and fantasy leagues. And who could pass up the chance to meet up in a chat room with Tiger Woods or Cal Ripken?

Brøderbund Clicks with Entertainment

Of all the computer software games to hit the market over the past two decades, none has created as great a stir—or generated as much revenue—as a pair released by Brøderbund Software, Inc. (www.brøderbund.com), in 1993 and 1997, respectively.

The first, a fantasy-oriented game called Myst, took players into mystical worlds where creativity and cunning were needed to solve the logic puzzles encountered in adventures that could last forty hours or more. A break from the high-speed, shoot-'em-up titles then swamping the market, Myst's refreshing premise and eye-catching graphics appealed to kids and adults alike. In less than five years, Myst sold nearly five million copies, generating more than $100 million in revenue.

Players begged for a follow-up.

Four years later they got their wish with Riven, the sequel to Myst. Featuring many of the same characters as its predecessor, Riven received tremendous pre-release hype and reached one million in sales faster than any software package in history except for Windows 95. When the market-analysis firm PC Data released its domestic sales figures for 1997, Riven and Myst held the top two spots for entertainment software—even though Riven had only been on store shelves for the final 62 days of the year.

But while Myst and Riven have proven commercial and critical windfalls for Brøderbund, they by no means represent its only major successes. The Novato, California–based enterprise—an affiliate of The Learning Company—has created or acquired the rights to some of the computer world's most popular educational and personal-productivity software.

It didn't take Brøderbund long to realize that the Internet was a perfect match for their offerings. The company created a Web site in 1996 that not only sold the full range of its products, but also included demo games, a bookstore, player chat rooms, and various other functions. "Gamers are an intense crowd, which translates very well to the Internet," explains Michael Murray, general manager of Brøderbund Online Business Unit. "They like technology. They upgrade their computers faster and more often than anybody else. They want to communicate with one another online. The Web is a natural progression for us." To handle this passionate and profitable niche, the company has created a gaming-software division—Red Orb Entertainment.

The growth of Brøderbund Software in many ways mirrors the evolution of computer-based entertainment as a whole. Conceived by brothers Doug and Gary Carlston, Brøderbund—its name is a two-language hybrid meaning "brotherhood"—was founded in 1980 just as PCs were starting to grow in popularity. The Carlstons would later declare a corporate vision of "creating interactive consumer experiences," but their initial goal was simply to market a pair of futuristic computer games—Galactic Empire and Galactic Trader—that Doug, a lawyer, had written in his spare time.

Once they saw the profit potential of Doug's work, the brothers made a full-time commitment to their company. They set up headquarters in Eugene, Oregon, formed an alliance with Japanese software maker StarCraft, and began selling a complete line of home entertainment products. With an eye toward diversification, they brought in their sister Cathy Carlston to serve as vice president of educational market planning.

By 1984 Brøderbund was selling millions of dollars worth of software annually and had relocated to Northern California's Marin County. It scored its first major hit with Print Shop, a personal productivity program that allowed users to design their own promotional pamphlets, banners, and signs using a variety of graphics and fonts. Print Shop went on to sell more than five million copies. This was followed up in 1985 by Where in the World Is Carmen Sandiego?, a game that helped children learn geography and history by chasing a crafty villain around the globe. It too proved hugely successful, and led to a popular children's TV show of the same name.

Gary and Cathy Carlston both left the organization in 1989, but Brøderbund continued to prosper and expand. Going public in 1991, the company acquired electronic atlas publisher PC Globe the following year and Banner Blue Software—producers of the top-selling genealogy software program Family Tree Maker—in 1995. Parsons Technology, makers of the Quicken series of home and office software that includes Quicken Family Lawyer and Quicken Estate Planner, was also brought into the fold.

"As a company, Brøderbund was following its vision of creating interactive consumer experiences," says Murray. "It started with games and then branched out into other areas—concentrating on those 'evergreen products' such as the Print Shop and Family Tree Maker that people could use over and over."

Building from the success of its Carmen Sandiego game, Brøderbund delved further into educational entertainment. In a joint venture with Random House, the company produced a series of interactive CD-ROMs known as "Living Books" that featured The Cat in the Hat and other Dr. Seuss classics. Quickly, Brøderbund became recognized as a leader in the growing field of "edutainment."

In the middle of all this came the Myst phenomenon. Designed by another two-brother team—Rand and Robyn Miller of software maker Cyan, Inc.—who partnered with Brøderbund, Myst was the first CD-ROM blockbuster. Knowing that only seven million American homes had CD-ROM access* at the time of its 1993 release, its creators expected sales of about 50,000 copies. But driven by Internet word of mouth, Myst quickly caught fire with the computer cognoscenti—and five million copies flew out the door.

"It was the best user experience at the time—we put in more animation, sound, and multimedia than anybody else," explains Murray. "During the four-year cycle time between Myst and Riven, the gaming industry grew up. Suddenly, intensive 3-D development was what was important, and Riven was right on the cusp of that. There were more frames of animation in Riven than there are in most movies."

Brøderbund's ascendancy was acknowledged by the Software Publishers Association, which honored the company with its 1998 awards for Best New Consumer Software (Riven), Best Overall Media Production (Riven), Best Home Education Software for Pre-Teens (Carmen Sandiego Word Detective), Best Curriculum Software for Middle Schools (Where in Time Is Carmen Sandiego?), and Best Home Productivity Software Program (Family Tree Maker Deluxe Edition III).

Murray estimates that 80 to 90 percent of Brøderbund's customers are Internet users, which has given the company a tremendous advantage in its attempts to establish an online presence. With a main Web site (www.brøderbund.com) linked to sites for Riven, Family Tree Maker, Parsons, and Red Orb, Brøderbund has more than two million online visitors each month.

"As far as games are concerned, people are coming online because they want to know what's new and what's coming, along with the most

*Gary Samuels, "CD-ROM's First Big Victim," Forbes, Feb. 28, 1994, p. 42.

recent tips and hints for improving their performance," says Murray. "They may also download upgrades, get technical support, or download demos of a new game they haven't tried yet. We have online demos for every one of our games."

Although these services are free, Brøderbund generated $10 million of its $300 millon in 1998 revenue from its Web sites—mostly through sales of new products. This was a 400 percent leap from 1997. After technology costs, royalties, depreciation, and the salaries of the thirty-odd people on its Internet staff, Brøderbund still makes close to a 30 percent profit margin online. While Internet sales are expected to increase dramatically, costs will level off—meaning even larger profits.

Brøderbund currently earns $100 million a year through all direct sources—the Internet, direct mail, and telephone orders—meaning that 10 percent of that is generated online. Murray would like to see that percentage increase.

A look at how the online revenue breaks down provides a good indication of what Internet customers are buying—and where marketing can be improved. Approximately 35 percent of revenue is generated through sales of new software, CD-ROMS, and other physical products; 25 percent originates from e-mails the online business unit sends out each month; 15 percent comes from content-oriented back-end services such as access to libraries and family archives; 15 percent comes from electronic software downloaded by customers; and 10 percent is sales through online sites other than Brøderbund.

Based on these findings, the company is building new revenue streams. As an example, Murray points to Brøderbund's genealogy site, www.familytreemaker.com. Amateur family sleuths, many of whom already own Brøderbund genealogy products, regularly congregate in the site's chat rooms to swap stories and tips for finding lost family members.

The site offers a host of other services, including family-finding tools and an "Online University" with classes such as "Tracing immigrant origins." There are also ads for the company's genealogy software—which can be ordered online—and links to Brøderbund's other sites.

"These genealogists are very intense about their hobby, just like the gamers are intense about their games," says Murray. "They're coming onto the site to talk with us and each other on a regular basis, so they know when a new version of something is coming. As a result, we wind up doing a lot of direct sales to them online. And we make 30 to 40 percent more on our online sales versus going through a retailer."

Brøderbund is working to master the buzz-building potential of the Web. In the months leading up to the release of Riven in October 1997, the company launched a campaign that e-mailed a dozen hardcore gamers telling them to go to the Web site of Riven's creators, Cyan, Inc. Once at the Cyan site, the gamers were shown a "Webcam" image of a cake that had the online address of the first Riven Web site (journals.riven.com) written on it in frosting. The result—over 15,000 hits at the Riven site in the first week.

To keep the excitement building, curiosity seekers were periodically fed puzzles that provided clues about the new game's content. When the game finally hit the market, a record-shattering 100,000 units were sold in its first week.

"By giving something challenging to the super-intense leading-edge users first, we created unprecedented electronic word-of-mouth," explains Murray. "People wound up coming to our site and signing up in advance for the game in hordes. Before Riven ever went out the door, we had generated a lot in sales."

The big question in the gaming world these days is when the action will move online. Murray believes that as far as high-content games like Myst and Riven are concerned, such a shift will take some time. Riven requires five CD-ROMs to play and requires roughly 3 gigabytes of multimedia—far too much for most PC users to download. This means that for the time being software sales of advanced games won't be negatively affected by the Internet. As Murray explains, "The multimedia is developing faster than the technology to download it."

Brøderbund has, however, made an effort to give its gamers a taste of what online action will be like. In addition to demos, the company has created a fully functional Online Game Zone that features games for all ages including Mudball Wall, Code Breaker, and Columbus Rescue. Another ready-to-play game, War Lords III, can be found at the Red Orb site; a player can compete solo or find opponents through the "game matching" feature.

"This is great for the players, and great for us from a business and marketing standpoint," says Murray. "We get to see what countries people are coming in from, how they play the game, how often they play, and how long they play. We wind up being better able to market to them."

Murray stressed that many of the costs associated with the company's Web site—such as building a data warehouse, an online store, and back-end systems—are largely one-time-only expenses. The key now is to keep coming up with fresh products to satisfy an increasingly demanding audience—and ward off online competitors.

"The edge is going to be in having a close link to customers. That comes from developing a brand, and building interaction with customers on a regular, repetitive basis. You need to position yourself with the customer, not just sell to them."

Brøderbund scored heavily with Myst and Riven, games that were pioneers and defined an industry. But the company did not rest on that success, extending its empire to include a wide range of software products. It is now poised to add the Internet to its arsenal of electronic tools for captivating—and capturing—an audience.

❑ *How Brøderbund clicks with entertainment:*

1. By using demo games and sophisticated "teaser" sites to build excitement and demand.
2. By developing a wide range of *edut*ainment games that appeal to different markets.
3. By developing cutting-edge games that attract cutting-edge users.
4. By building an Internet infrastructure with low maintenance cost.

Berkeley Systems Clicks with Entertainment

Most high-tech players in the gaming market don't begin life with a federal grant. Nor do they start out in an attic. Berkeley Systems (www.berkeleysystems.com) did both. In 1987, Wes Boyd, an academic at the University of California at Berkeley, received federal money to develop a computer-based communication product for the visually impaired. Around this same time, Jack Eastman, a colleague looking for a diversion from his Ph.D. research into particle physics, wrote the program for the now classic Flying Toasters screen saver.

Eastman brought his airborne appliances to Boyd's fledging company, Berkeley Systems. It was a perfect match. Realizing they were onto a visually entertaining product that solved the problem of phosphorus burn-in, Boyd and Eastman set about building an entire product category—screen savers.

Screen savers proved an immediate hit and Berkeley Systems increased its revenues from $4 million to $28 million in less than four years. In 1993, when the market had reached its saturation point, the company broadened its reach into pure entertainment. Although its first foray—the game Triazzle—wasn't a commercial success, Berkeley Systems was committed to leveraging its solid reputation and consumer loyalty to establish a second franchise.

After several trials and errors, Berkeley Systems launched a product in 1995 that propelled it into the top realm of entertainment software creators. You Don't Know Jack began life as an educational game designed to support middle-school curricula. It quickly evolved—through a partnership between Berkeley and Jellyvision, a Chicago-based production company—into a CD-ROM entertainment for grown ups.

The game pits players against each other in a rush to answer trivia and pop-culture questions delivered by an irreverent, wise-cracking host. As on Jeopardy! and other TV quiz shows, players "buzz in" when they think they know the answer. Focusing on events of the past thirty years, You Don't Know Jack was an instant hit with the 20-to-40 set—and still is today. Since its October 1995 debut, it has sold over 1.2 million copies in seven different versions.

While launching Jack, Berkeley Systems' general manager Chris Deyo and his team were also pondering the company's future. Their concern stemmed from the recognition that the CD-ROM business is a modest growth industry. "It'll probably grow anywhere from 10 to 35 percent each year," says Deyo, "but there's a real glut of supply. There is just not enough retail space out there for every product to be successful. You Don't Know Jack could have been a one-trick pony, but it had legs—good staying power—and we wanted to work hard to leverage that property and create a consumer franchise around it."

The company began to research how best to employ the Net. "We soon realized that the Internet would be an even better delivery vehicle for our product than CD-ROMS were," says Deyo. "Our model for You Don't Know Jack had always been a television game show, and the Internet was much closer to that type of format than a CD-ROM."

Berkeley soon realized that the Internet has some notable advantages over television, too. First and foremost is interactivity—the ability of users to have real-time give and take with the games and with other players. Then there's the fact that consumers can set their own hours—without the hassle of a VCR. It's entertainment on demand. And games on the Internet don't have to conform to rigid thirty- or sixty-minute formats.

What the Web does share with television is the ability to deliver advertising. "Our entire business model is ad-supported," explains Deyo. "We found, however, that traditional Internet advertising—banner ads—are often gangly and unpolished. It hinders the entertainment experience when you're trying to play a game and some guy is trying to hawk you something across the bottom of the page." Mimicking television once again, the company developed ads that appear between game segments rather than on top of them.

Berkeley Systems launched its entertainment site—www.Bezerk.com—in late 1996. The site includes three games: You Don't Know Jack the netshow, You Don't Know Jack Sports the netshow, and Acrophobia. The latter, added in November 1997, is an interactive word game that pits players against the clock and each other in an effort to solve acronyms. Matches take place in hundreds of different "rooms," where up to fourteen people can chat while they play.

Full-screen ads appear at regular intervals throughout all three games, complete with dynamic sound and animation. In You Don't Know Jack the netshow, for instance, nine ads are displayed during each fifteen-minute game—two or three at a time—with each lasting between eight and twelve seconds. These are pure advertisements, not hyperlinks to other Web pages. And since they take place during breaks in the action, they have the undivided attention of players.

Berkeley Systems' commercials—the first of their kind on the Internet—are geared to maximize customer interest. If players are attracted to a product, they need only to hit any key on their keyboard during the ad. At the end of the game they're provided with a customized page touting the benefits of the products they picked.

In late 1997, Berkeley Systems commissioned research firm Mb*interactive* to evaluate the effectiveness of this type of advertising. The results: "These ads are twice as effective as Web banners, two and a half times as effective as television, and a third more effective than print ads, in terms of conveying a message that is recalled in association with the brand." Brand awareness went up from 96 percent in the control group to 99 percent in the test group, and the study also revealed the desirable demographics of the Bezerk audience—young, educated, and affluent.

Berkeley Systems' site has already attracted the advertising dollars of numerous high-profile companies including U.S. Robotics, Infoseek, Twenti-eth Century Fox, TBS Superstation, JAMTV/Rolling Stone, Visa, and Epson. However, despite the encouraging findings many large companies have yet to make substantial buys. For this to change, in Deyo's opinion, nontechnology companies will need to make a commitment to the medium.

"I believe the adoption rate will continue to grow and even accelerate," Deyo predicts. "There will be substantially increased spending in 1999. The more we are able to offer them impressive figures on the number of impressions their ad will get, the better."

While Berkeley Systems continues to generate 90 percent of its revenues from CD-ROM sales, it expects substantial online profits within the next year. The popularity of the Bezerk site, for instance, is growing. In the first twelve months after its launch more than two million games were played, and by mid-1998 the site boasted upwards of 600,000 registered users. About 25,000 games of Acrophobia—lasting an average of forty minutes each—are now played per day, and in February 1998 approximately 240,000 games of You Don't Know Jack the netshow were played.

With these kinds of numbers, Berkeley Systems appears well positioned to demonstrate the unique value of "netvertising," and to capitalize on it.

❏ *How Berkeley Systems clicks with entertainment:*

1. By revolutionizing the way advertising is delivered on the Web.
2. By creating a company personality that is friendly, funny, and irreverent.
3. By mimicking the excitement of television game shows—and then adding the boost of real-time interactivity.

IBM Clicks with Entertainment

During the sixteen days of the 1998 Winter Olympics in Nagano, Japan, not all the great seats were in the stands or in front of a television set. In fact a computer console may have provided the ultimate view. The official Olympic Web site hosted by IBM (www.nagano.com) received a total of 646.3 million hits over the course of the Games. On the seventh day (February 13) alone there were nearly fifty-seven million hits; by day fourteen, hits were coming in at a rate of 103,429 per minute. More people wound up "watching" the Olympics on the Internet than on television.

What was the reason for this phenomenon? For one thing, the Internet coverage offered advantages that TV couldn't match: news in real time, as events unfolded, with scores and final results posted instantly. What's more, the Internet enabled viewers to focus on those events or athletes they were interested in without time delays and commercials—or the extended profiles that television networks favor. Fans could even post messages to their favorite athletes, and IBM set up a "Surf Shack"—outfitted with thirty of its Aptiva laptops—where athletes could go online and answer their admirers.

Probably the most powerful pull of the site was its ability to let fans make an immediate and personal connection to the Games—their way. This was something television coverage simply couldn't offer. Some analysts went so far as to say that the site's popularity foretold the future of entertainment. From a public relations standpoint, IBM reaped enormous rewards.

IBM *earned* its accolades—and proved its mastery of Web technology. By the time the Games were finished the site had processed 4.5 terabytes of information (a terabyte is 1,000,000,000 bytes, the next level up from gigabytes), provided news feeds to eight global press agencies, enabled the transmission of 250,000 messages between athletes and their fans, and had done it all using complex multimedia applications in a user-friendly, eye-pleasing way. It was an impressive technological feat and an invaluable experience for IBM.

"The main reason we get involved in event sponsorships like Nagano or the U.S. Open is that these events draw a huge amount of traffic in a very short period of time," explains Karl Salnoske, general manager of IBM's electronic commerce group. "The primary lessons we learned from Nagano were the ability to load balance across multiple sites while still giving the user the perception of a single site, to ramp-in additional servers as more capacity is needed, and to do it all very seamlessly with a high consistency in performance and response time."

Many of the features used by IBM were developed two or three years before, then tested in events such as the Deep Blue–Garri Kasparov chess match. The company was well prepared for the Nagano deluge and its success has led to commercial applications of the technology, most notably in its WebSphere Application Server and Performance Pack, released in June 1998.

Not one of the nearly 650 million hits generated by the Nagano site sold a single IBM product—at least not directly. The site's masthead carried the names and logos of the Nagano Olympic Organizing Committee and IBM, and if you clicked on the IBM logo you were linked to a site that provided additional information about the company as the "Official Internet Information Systems Provider to the Games." That site offered yet another link, this one to IBM's home page—www.ibm.com/shop. It was a pretty soft sell.

As soft as it was, however, the technological wizardry of the site was a fairly dramatic image-maker. Or image-changer—for a company that sorely needed it. Nagano was a showcase for the new IBM: a flexible provider of information technology, a savvy devisor of Internet solutions, and a company that has mastered the art of delivering electronic entertainment.

❏ *How IBM clicks with entertainment:*

1. By matching highly sophisticated technology with snappy graphics and sound—turning information into entertainment.
2. By allowing users to create their own entertainment experience, free of the limitations of television.
3. By reworking its image through an entertainment medium.

CBS Sportsline Clicks with Entertainment

When the Chicago Bulls wrapped up their sixth National Basketball Association championship in 1998, the partying continued long after the final buzzer sounded. Not only in the streets of the Windy City, but on millions of computer screens throughout the world. All night long Bulls fans celebrated on the Internet—trading electronic high fives, reading game analyses and interviews, and watching video replays of Michael Jordan's title-winning shot. They voted on whether or not they thought Jordan was going to retire, and purchased championship hats and tee shirts by the bundles. Exhausted by Bulls Mania, they could usher in the dawn by catching up on some baseball and hockey news.

The locale was the CBS SportsLine Web site (www.cbssportsline.com), which has fast become one of the top sports sites on the Internet.

Jam-packed with up-to-the-minute coverage of professional and amateur sports, the site offers its nearly one million daily visitors the real-time information, breaking news, critical insights, and sports-related products they crave. They can also join fellow fans in hundreds of different chat rooms, often for exclusive Q&As with star athletes. All told, the site contains more than 300,000 continuously updated pages.

CBS SportsLine has become the flagship site of SportsLine USA, Inc., a company founded in 1994 by entrepreneur Michael Levy. SportsLine was launched on the Internet in August 1995, manned by a staff of thirty. Today SportsLine USA employs more than 250 at its corporate offices in Fort Lauderdale, Florida, and has added sites dedicated to sports gambling (VegasInsider) and soccer (Soccernet), and home pages for a variety of superstar athletes including Michael Jordan, Tiger Woods, Shaquille O'Neal, Joe Namath, and Cal Ripken. There is even Internet-only sports talk radio that can be heard over computers.

According to Andy Sturner, vice president of business development for SportsLine USA, the company's goal is to create a "one-stop-shop" for sports fans online. Financing has come from a number of companies with a strategic interest in the success of the site, including Intel, Reuters, and TCI. In March 1997 Sportsline USA entered into a five-year partnership with CBS Sports. In exchange for giving CBS a 19 percent stake in the company and changing the name of its primary site to CBS SportsLine, Sportsline will receive more than $57 million in advertising and promotion on CBS Sports broadcasts through 2001. In addition, CBS has the option to acquire additional equity in Sportsline USA.

The site has built up a corps of nearly seventy-five full-time editors and journalists, supplemented by a network of freelance writers from around the country. As Sturner explains it, the company is attempting to establish a branded franchise—the first place people go on the Internet to satisfy their craving for sports. It markets itself to advertisers as the ideal interactive environment in which to reach fans before, after, and even during major sporting events.

"SPLN is building the third great U.S. sports brand," says Sturner. "The two most recognized brands in existence today are ESPN (the all-sports network) on television and *Sports Illustrated* in print. They are the standard by which all others are judged. Our goal is to become the leading interactive brand."

Based on increased usage and revenue growth during its first three years, CBS SportsLine appears to be taking solid steps towards its objective. First quarter figures for 1998 showed that daily visits were up more than 400 percent—127,000 versus 656,000—from the previous year. Revenue for 1998 was expected to be around $30 million—a leap of 250 percent from 1997's $12 million. Costs are expected to remain relatively flat.

The main revenue stream is advertising sales, which accounted for nearly two thirds ($4 million) of the $6.6 million generated during the first quarter of 1998. In cooperation with CBS television's sales force, CBS SportsLine coordinates its advertising and sponsorship packages around sporting events such as the Daytona 500,the Olympics, the NCAA Final Four, and college and professional football. Sponsors include American Express, Coca Cola, and Ford.

The reason for CBS SportsLine's appeal to advertisers is clear: as well as providing superstar endorsers, the site is geared to a very desirable demographic—affluent, educated males ages eighteen to forty-nine. Because the site is operational twenty-four hours a day, seven days a week, advertisers know they can reach this audience at work and at home, morning and night.

"Think about it," poses Sturner. "How does an advertiser reach this highly attractive demographic from 9:00 A.M. to 7:00 P.M. Monday through Friday? They are all at the office. It's all about access. With us, advertisers can reach these men during their lunch hour or between meetings, when they sign on and check out scores. In fact, one of our two biggest usage periods every day is between 12:00 P.M. and 2:00 P.M."

The lunch-hour factor speaks directly to the great appeal and secret weapon of the Internet: timing and timeliness. Fans can get their sports fix anywhere anytime in real time—even while a game is still in progress. Depth of information is another unique plus. If a baseball fanatic wants to know who played shortstop for the Cubs in 1936, he can click on the site's search engine and get his answer.

The biggest reason for the site's popularity, however, may be the jolt of excitement it provides. Sports fans are a dedicated bunch who just can't get enough. With CBS SportsLine they can chat with other enthusiasts online while watching a game on TV. And if they can't get the game on TV, they can link into "virtual stadiums" for animated play-by-play accounts. "For the displaced fan, Baseball Live! is perfect," explains Sturner. "For example a New York Yankees fan living in Florida can literally follow every pitch of a game on our site for free."

CBS SportsLine has developed another revenue stream by offering membership opportunities. For $4.95 per month, members receive inside scoops, interviews, exclusive columns, reference materials, discounts on dining, hotels, and travel worldwide, and 10 percent off all items sold in the site's Sports Store. They can also create their own personalized home page, filled with links to the sports, teams, and athletes most important to them. By the first quarter of 1998 CBS SportsLine had already signed up fifty thousand members, who accounted for $500,000 in revenue. "Our membership growth is very important," says Sturner. "It is creating a sense of community for the users of the site."

CBS SportsLine has also established strategic partnerships with America Online, Excite, and Microsoft Internet Explorer in an effort to raise its online profile. Competing primarily with two other network-backed Web sites—ESPN Sportszone and CNNSI—it held the top spot in the February 1998 MediaMetrix ratings. After its initial public offering in November 1997, SportsLine's share price more than doubled in two months.

"As access speeds increase," says Sturner, "you're going to see more multimedia content, more audio and video, a more dynamic and compelling experience. But it all starts with the quality of the content itself. Of course you need strong technology and distribution in place, but nothing matters if you don't have the best content. In that sense, we're right where we want to be."

CBS SportsLine is in the game to win—and it has built a team with great depth of talent to make sure it does.

❑ *How CBS clicks with entertainment:*

1. By bringing the excitement of sports to life on the Web.
2. By tapping into a lucrative demographic—affluent men between the ages of eighteen and forty-nine.
3. By coordinating its advertising with CBS television.

How You Can Click with Entertainment

- By making your site easy on the eyes, clever, well written, exciting. Many of today's graphic designers are real artists capable of turning the Web into a magical world of color and movement. Similarly, use writers who can establish a rapport with users. Keep your site friendly and personal—strive to make a connection.

- By dazzling, thrilling, and keeping it fast. Today's young shoppers have grown up in a world where the lines between entertainment and commerce are blurred, if not totally erased. Make your product a part of the action, a must-have for young scenemakers (and scenemaker wannabes).
- By putting your product or service in the context of family and community, caring and continuity. Wrap it in a warm and comforting glow. Don't only look to sell a message; try telling a story.
- By never underestimating the power of whimsy and humor. The overall message of clicking with entertainment is to make the experience fun, interesting, a journey.

9

Click with Trust

Build trust.
Boost profits.

It isn't easy to entrust your credit card number to some unseen, voiceless electronic wave that seems to be connected to billions of strangers.

That the Internet may not at first inspire trust is certainly understandable, particularly in light of widely published media alarms about hackers and Internet security. That hundreds of companies and millions of customers have by now in fact learned to make the Internet eminently trustworthy is the subject of this chapter.

One of the Internet's great virtues is its openness, which encourages relationships between multitudes of individuals and organizations. But the Web provides users a measure of anonymity that translates into a certain degree of uncertainty, if not outright distrust.

Before launching a Web site, a company should resolve some trust issues. What can it do to make its customers feel comfortable when handing over money, and sometimes a great deal of money, to a faceless recipient in a new and faceless environment? Can it demonstrably ensure the honesty and quality its customers expect? And can it do this so effectively that millions of hits turn into millions of dollars in sales?

In this chapter, three companies address these questions: Metropolitan Life Insurance Company, Wells Fargo & Company, and Charles Schwab & Company.

MetLife, as it is often called, has spiced up its site with services and information that emit a sense of concern for every customer's welfare. Met visitors can go through an "Insurance 101" primer, which includes a self-assessment guide that enables them to figure out what insurance they need. On the "Life Advice Exchange" bulletin board, they can swap stories about everything from getting married to getting ready for retirement.

Wells Fargo embraced the Internet before any other major bank, and it continues to rank among the leading online financial institutions. Its Web site allows users to handle their bank accounts, pay their bills, and buy or sell stocks—all online. The site also offers a rich menu of money advice, including weekly commentaries on the U.S. economy.

Securities broker Charles Schwab, after executing discount trades electronically for more than a decade, now aims to become the Internet version of a full-service brokerage house. Customers traveling to Schwab's site can get real-time stock quotes, catch up on the latest economic news and trends, or calculate how much they will need in savings to retire or pay for a child's college education.

In developing their Web sites, all these companies resolved the trust issue by ensuring privacy for their customers and educating them about the Internet's ease and efficiency.

By showing that this new medium can actually offer the same high level of service and confidentiality their customers have long grown used to, MetLife, Wells Fargo, and Charles Schwab eliminate the apprehension their customers may have about going online.

MetLife Clicks with Trust

It may seem an odd coupling—an insurance company and the Internet. After all, insurers evoke an image of conservatism and personal customer relationships, and that's a far cry from the anonymous, fast-changing infobahn. But Metropolitan Life Insurance Company of New York, better known as MetLife (www.metlife.com), is bridging the gap between Internet and insurance. Its ally in the quest to transfer trust to an electronic medium is the company's mascot, Snoopy, a character whose appeal spans generations. The bemused beagle—shown riding a surfboard or working at a computer terminal—is joined on MetLife's Web site by Charlie Brown, Pig Pen, and other members of the loved and trusted *Peanuts* comic strip gang. The message is clear: We're still MetLife and we're still here for our customers.

Founded in 1868 in New York City, MetLife is one of the world's largest financial services companies, with more than $330 billion in assets and millions of clients worldwide. The company has more than 45,000 associates who provide or administer life, health, and property/casualty insurance. It also offers savings, retirement, and a range of other financial products and services for both individuals and groups.

The company's Web site—MetLife Online—was established in December 1995 and is widely acknowledged as the top insurance site on the Internet. It has garnered numerous awards, including the coveted "double sunglasses" rating from the Yahoo! search engine company. The site has also become an increasingly popular destination, with the number of visitors growing from 375,000 a year in 1996 to 500,000 a month by the middle of 1998.

While the *Peanuts* gang gives the site a friendly and easygoing identity, the move to the Internet marks a major change in corporate culture and interdepartmental cooperation. The relationship between MetLife's Information Technology and Internet Operations units has always been strong, but the sustained success of the site has been the result of unprecedented teamwork across the company. Departments from Legal to Customer Service to Advertising collaborate closely both to get the mileage each needs from the site and to give it a uniform feel for visitors.

The move online represents a major adjustment in how MetLife relates to its customers. The company built its reputation on thousands of salespeople, who for generations have sat at customers' dining room tables and patiently sold them security blankets for all of life's major transitions. How does an organization translate that trust to a fast and faceless electronic medium? Instead of knocking on customers' doors, MetLife is inviting customers to knock on its door. That the company has managed not only to maintain but to enhance its customers' faith and confidence is testament to its Web commitment and savvy.

The company has always been technology friendly. It began using interactive video kiosks to sell products in 1993. When the Internet took hold, the company knew it wanted to have an online presence. One major question was whether to go via a dial-up service such as Prodigy, CompuServe, or AOL—which is how some companies made their Internet debuts during the mid-1990s—or to go directly onto the Web. After studying the question, MetLife decided it would reach more people more readily and at less expense on the Web.

Because of a variety of constraints, most major insurance companies aren't yet selling insurance directly online. Instead, they're providing information about major choices people make in their lives. MetLife focuses on selling "trust" rather than a specific product. Visitors can learn about insurance products, then e-mail a request for a sales rep to call them. The site's Life Advice Center—a combination information center, bulletin board, and chat room—offers a forum for giving or getting advice about retirement investing, saving for college, financial issues relating to divorce, and credit problems. There are tips on staying cool when your teenager gets her driver's license, how to handle a child's first day at school, and how to deal with both the practical and emotional aspects of moving into a new house. Visitors also peruse a gallery of baby photos and share concerns from the prosaic to the profound. By helping people through an IRS audit, the breakup of a marriage, or the arrival of twins, MetLife hopes to win them as customers.

"We had a very deliberate strategy of building strong relationships based on trust and on educating the consumer," says Richard L. Painchaud, vice president in charge of interactive commerce at MetLife. "The Life Advice program is very much an integral component of this strategy. We hope to engage customers and eventually sell them insurance and other financial products. The subjects we cover are the day-to-day events that we're all faced with. Our major online categories are family, insurance, money, health, business, and purchases. Our site is committed to allowing people to participate in communities that are focused around seventy-one different life events." The idea is to create "pockets" within the overall site that the visitors feel they own, and where they can post and retrieve information relevant to their lives.

Among the most popular features of the MetLife site are the tables that visitors can use to measure their height and weight against U.S. norms and check out other vital signs of good health and longevity. Other tools include a mortgage calculator and a moving distance calculator. Additional features are on the way, each designed to further deepen customers' comfort level with MetLife as an organization that can help them lead fuller lives.

The site proudly displays MetLife's membership in the Insurance Marketplace Standards Association (IMSA). Created to promote high standards of ethical conduct, the IMSA requires that an organization undergo a rigorous independent evaluation to qualify. MetLife was one of the first companies to meet these standards, a fact it clearly points out on its site—right alongside a listing of the IMSA's six principles of ethical market conduct.

MetLife's retail and institutional customers have different needs and the company has taken steps to address them. MetLife's business-to-business section allows corporate visitors to go into a section called "My personal Met," where they can essentially create their own mini-Web site. A consultant can go into the site and get help setting up a plan for a client with ten thousand employees and a pension package of $100 million, for instance. On the other hand, individual customers can contact the company, make inquiries, seek out a sales associate, or review a personal insurance policy.

The site has private access links to its major corporate clients—a feature that holds particular promise as a revenue producer. One such extranet now in operation allows employees of Microsoft Corporation to access their MetLife insurance and pension plans twenty-four hours a day. And when they are ready to buy or change a policy, they can call a MetLife representative and complete their application in a matter of minutes.

MetLife is able to track buying patterns among users, data that can be turned into valuable marketing strategies. The company does not, though, ever release information about personal matters such as salary and marital status.

Based on feedback from customers and employees, MetLife launched a revised site in early 1998. The improvements include more intuitive icons and more explanations of content. There's also less scrolling needed to get at information, and a navigation bar at the bottom of each page lends consistency across the site. Currently, the company is spending less than the cost of one television commercial to both advertise the site *and* keep it running. MetLife is proving how cost effective the Internet can be.

With an ever-growing number of visitors showing their trust in the organization by moving online, MetLife is in the position to capture new revenue streams and profits.

❏ *How MetLife clicks with trust:*

1. By avoiding the hard sell, preferring to offer reliable real-life information that site visitors can use to help them through life's transitions.
2. By opening up the site to honest dialog not only between the company and customers, but between customers.
3. By respecting the confidentiality of customers' personal information.

Wells Fargo Clicks with Trust

The first duty of any bank is to ensure that its customers' money is handled, transferred, and accounted for safely and accurately. In the design of its Internet site, Wells Fargo & Company (www.wellsfargo.com) kept this duty uppermost in its mind. It created a site that delivers bank products and services securely and efficiently. At the same time, the site saves the bank money and positions it to attract new customers from the growing online population.

With assets of well over $196 billion, Wells Fargo offers a full spectrum of financial services and has a long reputation as being a company of the highest integrity. It went online in 1989 and in 1995 became the first major bank to offer its retail customers Internet banking. Wells Fargo Online has led its industry—being heralded as the standard setter by Time Digital Financial Net News and the Online Banking Association. At the end of 1998, 700,000 Wells Fargo customers banked over the Internet.

The company's success flies in the face of pervasive myths about the Internet. Many consumers still believe that the Web is a porous place, risky even for inexpensive credit card purchases. In fact, Wells Fargo and other companies have constructed secure sites that protect transaction integrity and confidentiality.

According to Dudley Nigg, the executive vice president who pioneered online financial services for Wells Fargo, the company recognized early on the opportunity presented by the Internet—and committed itself aggressively. And statistics now show that customers are responding with commitment of their own; customers with online accounts are more loyal.

Customers log onto Wells Fargo's site and, after entering their password, immediately gain access to their accounts. They can transfer funds, apply for new accounts, buy travelers' checks and foreign currency, download information into personal financial-management software, and pay bills. "Bill presentment" will be added to the site. This feature will present to online customers bills and associated detail. Online customers will have the option to pay the bills electronically rather than by mail.

Wells Fargo has methodically addressed the issues of security and privacy; indeed, the site provides detailed information about its privacy policy, encryption technology, and other security measures, to assure customers they are banking with a leader in Internet security. Nigg says that a big challenge for the company is changing the public's perception about whether they could confidently conduct Internet transactions.

"Ignorance was a far bigger issue than security itself," said Nigg. "Our real challenge was—and still is—to educate customers. We need to make people aware of how safe the medium is, and the advantages it provides." Those advantages include speed, ease of use, and the up-to-the-minute accuracy of the information. Customers can manage their own finances on their own time.

Industry studies have shown that in terms of the bottom line, the Internet is astonishingly attractive. The cost of serving a customer who comes into a branch averages one dollar. Handling an ATM transaction costs twenty cents. The cost of an online transaction is one cent—a penny.

In light of those figures, it's hardly surprising that the competition is growing. Citibank has shifted focus from its proprietary software to Internet banking, and is looking to encourage a sense of community on its Web site. Bank of America has developed a content-rich site that features detailed information on personal finance options. Chase Manhattan uses charts to illustrate account information.

No other bank, however, has made the transition online as quickly or aggressively as Wells Fargo. It has always been an innovative company— a leader in modernizing branches, offering phone services, and moving into grocery stores. And with its vision of offering services such as bill presentment, Wells Fargo has taken the lead in making the online bank a tool for more than basic services. The company has 15 million customers overall and Nigg believes that "50 percent—up from the current 8 percent to 10 percent—of them will be banking online in the next five to ten years."

The start-up costs were substantial, but Wells Fargo believes that the cost per transaction will decline due to vastly increased usage. "We have," Nigg says, "been able to add more technology at the front end with less support at the back end." This translates into a dramatic reduction in the cost per customer.

Most online customers are established ones—the Internet isn't garnering the company new business. But the fact that existing customers can be better served—with increasing loyalty—is a fine result.

In the future, Wells Fargo predicts that customers will be visiting their online bank as regularly as their mailbox. Nigg is convinced that the bank "will be able to leverage this relationship to offer more products and a broader range of services—brokerages, loans, buying a car, travel, you name it."

Wells Fargo Online is proving that even in the most trust-based industries, the Internet can provide solutions that are better for the company and the customer. The technology can be trusted to work, and customers can be educated to embrace its efficiencies even in sensitive transactions.

❏ *How Wells Fargo clicks with trust:*

1. By using sophisticated encryption technology to create a site that is secure and confidential.
2. By strengthening the company's long history of customer loyalty based on a faith in its ability to protect and manage money.
3. By placing detailed information on security measures and policy on the site.

Charles Schwab Clicks with Trust

On May 1, 1975, the Securities and Exchange Commission abolished the fixed-rate brokerage commission, and the brokerage house Charles Schwab and Company (www.schwab.com) opened for business armed with banks of telephones. Its goal was to enable investors to buy and sell stocks over the phone at astonishingly low prices. In exchange for the low fees, customers left behind personal hand holding, which was fine with them. They wanted the low prices. This represented a dramatically new equation—the beginning of the discount revolution in the brokerage industry. Schwab continued to lead the charge, building a network of branches that recruited customers right off the street with the same promise: bare-bones service and low cost.

Offering software for computer-based trading without the need for company interaction was a natural evolution of this principle. Schwab's DOS-based "Equalizer" debuted in 1985, and was followed by the Windows-based "Street Smart" in 1993. The establishment of a Web site in 1995 was the next step.

But investors familiar with Schwab's no-frills reputation are in for a surprise the first time they log onto www.schwab.com. Using Net technology, the company is offering a wealth of information and services. Within the site's Analyst Center, clients have access to research from Dow Jones, Standard & Poor, Big Charts, Market Guide, and First Call. At the Schwab Investor Tax Center, clients will find an online IRA analyzer, a capital gains estimator, explanations of the 1997 Tax Relief Act, year-end tax tips, tax strategies for the year ahead, and a tax forecasting worksheet.

Schwab's Mutual Fund Marketplace and Mutual Fund OneSource give clients direct access to—and comparative ratings of—more than 1,500 funds from 215 families. MarketBuzz offers market information from a wide range of sources. The Asset Allocation Toolkit lets customers categorize their holdings by asset class and compare them to other allocation strategies. The College Saver Program provides tuition-building options that factor in the age of the child and individual tolerances for risk. The Investment Forum, presented through Excite and iVillage, puts investors in direct touch with industry experts.

"Schwab's goal is to give customers a complete investing experience," says Gideon Sasson, president of electronic brokerage for Charles Schwab. "For the first time, customers have access to the same powerful tools as traditional brokers."

All of this adds up to what Schwab's co-CEO David S. Pottruck calls "a new era for Schwab, not as a discount broker, but as a major force in redefining full service." And the good news for Schwab customers is that the discount part of the equation hasn't disappeared. Although its rates are higher than those of recent entrants to the online brokerage market, Schwab charges $29.95 for any trade up to one thousand shares (and three cents per share thereafter), which is substantially less than traditional full-service firms charge. While deep-discount brokers may charge 40 to 60 percent less than Schwab, they don't offer nearly the same level of Internet-based services.

What's more, Schwab opened thirty-seven new branch offices in the United States last year, bringing its total to 280. The branches help novice investors develop a strategy based on age, risk tolerance, time horizons, and other variables. The typically more sophisticated online investors seek a different level of consultation. The wealth of information on the Schwab Web site enables them to understand their portfolios and to develop comprehensive strategies. When these investors need help on complex issues, their questions are informed and to the point. This is where Schwab's seasoned, savvy advisors can provide expert assistance.

"There is no way we can manage our business without our brokers or branch offices," says Sasson. "Technology can only take the customer so far. The ability to convey complex information in a technological environment is limited. This is serious money people are dealing with, and human interaction is essential at times. People need help with concepts, and as a company we need educated employees to provide that help. If I want to sell twenty thousand shares of IBM, I don't want to do that online. I want to know I'm talking in person to someone who understands my expectations of how to manage the trade and take it to the floor for me. I want someone I can trust."

This evolution of Schwab into a largely online, personally supported incarnation of the full service brokerage has been swift. The ability to offer online customers refined, directed information has been a key driver of that evolution. The mass movement of investors—as opposed to pure traders—onto the Internet has been another driver. "Online has become the backbone of the business," says Sasson.

In 1997, Schwab's online business grew by more than 90 percent, to

1.2 million accounts with $81 billion in assets. Online trades grew to 37 percent of total trades, up from 25 percent the year before. By the middle of 1998, online trades were up to 50 percent of the company total. In just the first three months of 1998, Internet trading attracted more than 350,000 new accounts representing $21 billion in assets. Schwab does more than twice the business of its nearest online competitor. In fact, according to Forrester Research, Schwab captures a 50 to 60 percent share of all online assets.

As far as the future is concerned, Schwab looks at its own 3 percent share of the $13 trillion of investable assets in the United States and sees plenty of room for growth. In the nearer term, the company has a stated goal of serving ten million households and attracting $1 trillion in customer assets by 2005. With three million households, 5.4 million individual accounts, and $430 billion in assets, it is a third of the way there. The company expects that the remaining two thirds will come almost entirely online.

Charles Schwab and Company has changed. The ascendancy of the Internet has both dictated these changes and made them possible. The company has shown that is able to seize opportunity without sacrificing trust.

❏ *How Charles Schwab clicks with trust:*

1. By growing from a no-frills brokerage into a full service online company without sacrificing low price.
2. By providing expert in-person support to answer complex investor questions and to perform large trades.
3. By maintaining the highest levels of efficiency and integrity online.

How You Can Click with Trust

- By offering useful information and colorful, humorous graphics up front—rather than a heavy sales pitch. By featuring a Web site that focuses more on making customers smile than selling them something right away, as MetLife does, a company can earn respect and trust.

- By earning your customers' trust. Everyone worries about the security of their money. Privacy issues—relating both to financial transactions and intimate relationships—are uppermost in the mind of all Americans these days, and many products deal with sensitive matters of health. Your job is to mitigate people's anxieties by promising and delivering discretion and security, as well as accuracy, reliability, and efficiency. If you make a pledge not to share customer information, stick to it. It is impossible to overstress the importance of this in building customer trust. Trust lost is difficult to regain, especially with so many competitors out there.

- By building on a trusting relationship—as Charles Schwab does—by offering new products and services that you stand behind with all of your established integrity. Once they feel secure, convince customers of the ease and convenience of conducting trust-sensitive business online.

Epilogue

This book was written to address the concerns of businesspeople who are thinking about how their companies might capture the Internet advantage. By reporting on the experience of Northwest Airlines, Cisco Systems, Dell Computer, Federal Express, and the other companies described here, our intent was to reveal the valid and significant business benefits they have achieved through their online ventures. These companies were selected to highlight the eight essential benefits that businesses are capturing to deliver a meaningful Internet advantage for their stakeholders—be they shareholders, customers, or business partners.

We don't think that the successes or the companies profiled here are singular or unique. Their achievements can be analyzed and described in ways that others can learn from. Their experience rebuts both misconceptions that have prevented some from taking steps toward meaningful online participation, and also high-flying rhetoric that would have you believe that achieving Internet success is as simple as asking a small group of smart, technology-wise employees to build the company's Web site.

As you read the stories of the companies presented here, we hope you began to think about how their experience and achievements could be successfully applied to your own company. As this book goes to print, at Arthur Andersen we have been working hard on our own Internet venture: a knowledge-management service named KnowledgeSpace (www.knowledgespace.com). It is designed as a powerful gateway to online business information, with resources designed to make the Internet more efficient and productive for business users. We are giving online subscribers access to many of the formerly proprietary diagnostic tools and insights from Arthur Andersen's Global Best Practices® knowledgebase, as well as many other business performance enhancement tools. This service integrates these deep resources with insights from Arthur Andersen professionals on the top business news each day. It also provides customized news reports from more than seventy-five newspapers, magazines, and journals, using the most comprehensive set of specific business search terms and concepts available in the market.

To help you move forward—a step we hope you will take soon—we would be remiss if we did not provide you with some thoughts on how to do so. Our approach begins with an invitation to examine your business and its context. This review might examine the following:

- *Company.* What is your mission? What are your key business processes? What information assets do you hold?
- *Customers.* What are their connectivity needs? What issues can they solve online?
- *Business partners.* How well do their business processes interoperate with yours?
- *Competitors.* How are they positioning their online efforts? Where are they succeeding? Are there any companies outside your industry that are implementing technologies that could be deployed to provide services to and diminish your relationships with your customers?
- *Industry.* Are standards emerging for Internet business?

It is clear that the Internet poses both an opportunity for and a threat to established businesses. Cisco provides a stunning example of what can be accomplished. It can articulate a range of savings garnered through internetworking and that can be converted to a tremendous competitive advantage. Barnes & Noble felt the threat of Amazon.com, a smart competitor that seized a strong first-mover advantage. We chose to share the efforts of Barnes & Noble, in part, because its commitment to succeed with barnesandnoble.com is meeting the challenge.

Next, explore your options:

- What are the Internet advantages that make sense in light of your business relationships?
- What advantages can you harness to extend your current offerings online or present new products and services?
- What people, processes, and technology resources will you need to capture those advantages?
- How will you align your existing processes to support your efforts?
- Who will champion the venture within your company?
- How will results be measured, recognized, and rewarded?

Many of the executives at the companies we interviewed focused our attention on the critical role top management played in the nascent stages of their online ventures. Expedia, for example, was able to change its scope and purpose with the support of Bill Gates. The online efforts of Marshall Industries, Barnes & Noble, and Charles Schwab were similarly spurred by top management. Other companies, like Coldwell Banker and BMG, initially stumbled, but then recovered by refocusing and aligning their efforts—anchoring them to broad-based company support.

Once target advantages are identified, there comes the critical stage of designing and building prototypes. Many of the companies we spoke

with supported their efforts with a clearly articulated software development effort. They stress the importance of market research and usability
testing. The need for good information design is acute. The user experience, they emphasize, must be supported by programming logic. There is
no place for bells and whistles that interfere, confuse, and weigh down
the user. Contrary to much popular wisdom, these companies point to
the effectiveness of telephone support to bolster their efforts. Northwest
Airlines also highlighted the importance of adopting a pricing strategy
that would attract users and reward desired behavior.

As the companies described in this book have shown, there is no particular secret involved. There are mistakes to be made and many paths to
success. At core, we think that all companies are presented with the opportunity to become a clickable company—a company that captures the
Internet advantages by clicking with the eight characteristics presented
in this book:

1. *Information.* Enable customers to retrieve information about products and services that was previously inaccessible or available only at
great cost and trouble.

2. *Choice.* Offer customers the opportunity to choose, and help them
make the best choice.

3. *Convenience.* By breaking down barriers of time and space, provide
customers convenience in a fundamentally different way.

4. *Customization.* Offer personalized attention and give customers the
opportunity to tailor products to fit their needs and wants.

5. *Savings.* Reduce your costs by using the Internet to streamline

processes, eliminate barriers and better control the supply chain, then pass these savings on to customers.

6. *Community.* Invite customers to join online communities. By focusing on their interests, experiences, and issues, you can effectively and efficiently offer your products and services to an audience that has already expressed an interest.

7. *Entertainment.* Offer users a unique and powerful medium for fun and interactive activities, then leverage the attraction.

8. *Trust.* Eliminate customer apprehension by showing that the Internet can provide the high levels of service and confidentiality they expect in important face-to-face transactions, while also providing ease of use and efficiency.

Visit our Web site at http://www.arthurandersen.com/clickable

Index

About the Authors

Jonathan Rosenoer is director, electronic commerce readiness, in Arthur Andersen's national computer risk management practice. Prior to this, he was managing director, strategic alliances, for Arthur Andersen Knowledge Enterprises, and he has spent most of the past decade working on the development of commercial online and Internet-based systems, concentrating on associated business risk and process issues. A nationally recognized authority on online business and legal issues, Mr. Rosenoer founded the CyberLaw section of America Online in 1992. As executive editor and director of marketing, western region, for Counsel Connect, the largest online service for the legal community, he produced the first accredited online legal education program. An attorney, Mr. Rosenoer is the author of *CyberLaw: The Law of the Internet* (Springer Verlag, 1997) and has published articles in numerous periodicals, including *Wired* magazine, *Ethics and Behavior, Policy Options,* and *The Computer Lawyer,* among others.

Douglas E. Armstrong is director of marketing and digital communications at Arthur Andersen Knowledge Enterprises. He also directs marketing and business development for The Virtual Learning Network and Knowledge-Space (www.knowledgespace.com), Arthur Andersen's award-winning electronic knowledge services, as well as leading the design and development of knowledgespace.com and arthuranderson.com, the firm's Web site. Since receiving his M.B.A. from the University of Illinois, Urbana-Champaign, Mr. Armstrong has presented at numerous conferences and seminars on Internet and knowledge-sharing issues, including the 1997 World Economic Forum (Davos, Switzerland), the World Economic Development Congress (Washington, D.C., and Hong Kong), and the Crossing International Borders seminar (Chicago, Illinois).

J. Russell Gates is a partner in the Chicago office of Arthur Andersen LLP and leads Arthur Andersen's computer risk management practice in North America. He is also the worldwide head of Arthur Andersen's electronic commerce risk consulting and assurance initiatives, with responsibility for developing and coordinating service offerings relating to various aspects of electronic commerce, including business alignment, EC business risk management, cryptography and public key/private key infrastructure, and other Internet security and control services. Mr. Gates is the coauthor of Arthur Andersen's Information Security Framework, and is also responsible for Arthur Andersen's involvement with the economist intelligence unit's "Managing Business Risks in the Information Age," a 1998 study focused on client/server deployment, enterprise-wide solutions, and interbusiness connectivity.